PR
ZEN & THE A

MW01004078

"The one book every disc golfer needs... If you only pick up one book on this list, make it this one... This is one of those books that will end up with highlighter and notes all over it as you read it again and again."
– Time Steward (Mind Body Disc Blog)

"It is a cool book to motivate and inspire you, speaking in terms that Disc Golfers can understand. Definitely check this book out."
– Bobby Brown (The Disc Golf Answer Man Podcast)

"Zen and the Art of Disc Golf is a perfect read anytime of the year to help your disc golf game...It's safe to say that you'll take something away from it and in the end, you'll take steps to being a better disc golfer with the knowledge you'll gain."
– Zach Parcell (All Things Disc Golf Blog)

"A potentially valuable tool in your quest for the Perfect Round."
– DiscGolfer Magazine

"A must read for any disc golfer."
– Hucking Aces Blog

"A super good read."
– Justin (The Disc Golf Show)

DISCS & ZEN

DISCS & ZEN

More Writings on Disc Golf and Life

_____

by Patrick McCormick

DISCS & ZEN:
MORE WRITINGS ON DISC GOLF AND LIFE
[BY PATRICK MCCORMICK]

Copyright (c) 2016 Patrick D McCormick
ISBN-13: 978-1540647450
ISBN-10: 1540647455

First Edition.

Request for permissions or general contact may be made via
email directly to the author at zendiscgolf@gmail.com

www.zendiscgolf.com

TABLE OF CONTENTS

FOREWORD

By Tim Steward

I'm a book guy. Probably more than I am a disc golf guy, and that's saying a lot. That is why when I started the Mind Body Disc disc golf blog a little over two years ago, I wanted a disc golf reading list to be a prominent part of it. There was a small problem, though. At that time, there really weren't any books specifically about disc golf. Not any worth reading, anyway. And definitely none that would help you with your game.

So, I proceeded to look through my home library and compiled a list of books that had positively impacted my disc golf game. Ball golf strategy, philosophy, and general sports psychology were the topics of choice. I put together a small list, posted it on my site, and announced this disc golf reading list to the world with a simple statement...

"Who says there are no books about disc golf?"

Little did I know that that sentence would lead to both finding an actual book about disc golf and the formation of a friendship that would change my disc golf and personal life for the better. That one statement caused this random guy from the Internet, Patrick McCormick, to reach out and share that he had, in fact, just completed writing a book about disc golf. It was to be a small, yet highly impactful volume that combined disc golf, psychology, and philosophy. He called it *Zen and the Art of Disc Golf*, and I couldn't wait to read it.

The following months saw the release of his book, a podcast that I ended up helping to cohost, and a movement that has positively changed the lives of many disc golfers.

Those same months also saw the development of a friendship between Patrick and myself that I value greatly. We both see books as essential to our personal development, and we share them with each other regularly. We both love disc golf (probably a little more than we should). We both view disc golf as a microcosm of life. We both see disc golf as a walking meditation that can help us gain clarity about our lives on and off the course.

There's an old saying:

"In ten years, you will be the exact same person you are

today with the exception of the people you've met and the books you've read."

I know I'm not alone when I say I have been changed for the better because I met Patrick McCormick and because I read his book.

When he asked me if I would write the introduction to this new book, *Discs & Zen*, I was more than honored. The book you hold in your hands is just as inspiring, just as insightful, and just as beneficial as the first. It will help you play better disc golf. It will help you perform better in life. And most importantly, it will make you think.

This is a book (much like the original) that's not meant to be read once and set on a shelf. It is a guidebook. It is a reference tool. It is something you will want to visit again and again. I expect my copy of this new book to become just as dog-eared, highlighted, and underlined as the original. I've probably read that first book at least 10 times. How could I not? It's a book about disc golf! Which brings me back to where I started...
Who says there are no books about disc golf? I certainly don't anymore. Now there are at least two that are more than worth your time.

So, sit back and enjoy the read. If you're anything like I am, you'll get inspired at various points throughout this book to stop reading and get out on the course. I encourage you to do just that. Put the book down, grab your discs, and head out to huck some plastic. I know for a fact that Patrick won't mind. In fact, I'd bet he would be surprised if you didn't.

After all, Patrick's message has always been clear: It all comes down to one simple thing... Just Throw.

- Tim Steward
      Mind Body Disc

INTRODUCTION

"There was a shopping mall.
Now it's all covered with flowers.
You got, you got it."

- Talking Heads - *(Nothing But) Flowers*

It has been almost two years since *Zen & The Art of Disc Golf* found its way into the hands of disc golfers worldwide, and as I sit here to type, I am looking around at all of the ways that writing that slim volume of disc golf wit and wisdom changed my life forever. Who would have known that a simple idea while playing a round of disc golf at my local park would become a seed that would flourish into what others have called "a movement" in the sport? I hesitate even writing that because the idea has always seemed a little strange to me. However, *Z&TAODG* (as it will be referred to from here on out) is not just something I am proud of, but something that has changed so many other people's lives, brought me into contact with some of the biggest names in disc golf, gained me newfound friends and cohorts, and literally has blessed me and my family in more ways than I can articulate to you in words.

When I began writing *Z&TAODG*, I was renting a townhouse with my wife near the Bayville Disc Golf Course in Virginia Beach. My wife and I had been married less than a year, and I was playing disc golf every morning except the days I was on shift as a Medic Firefighter at a local fire department. Today, I am writing to you from my brand new office in my new home on an almost nine acre property near Gloucester, Virginia. I have been promoted to Lieutenant in the fire department. My wife gave birth to just about the coolest baby boy that this Earth has ever known, and I can't play a public round of disc golf without being flagged down to sign a book or a disc. (There are worse problems an author could have.) About the only thing that has remained the same are the camouflage shorts I refuse to retire and will be wearing when I turn 85. (Don't worry, I wash them from time to time.)

Within the past few months, my family and I have uprooted ourselves from our familiar suburban lifestyle and have transplanted to a small town, opting for country living and a more simple existence. We have sacrificed the everyday conveniences of shopping centers and three minute drives to Starbucks (although I can still drive an hour to get my cold brew fix if necessary) in order to create a lifestyle that fits us, and more importantly, to build a disc golf course that yours truly can live on.

Much like my first book, this lifestyle change began with the seed of an idea, a question actually: what do I really want out of this life? Not "What do I want in the future?", but "What can I make happen right now that would be my version of 'living the dream'?" I could not have made this move happen without *Z&TAODG*, without the blessings the book has given our family and more importantly, without living by the philosophies in the book. It is important that I note immediately, however, that we did all this without becoming millionaires, and in fact, we spend less money monthly than we did in our previous suburban life. It all began with forming a desire, believing it was possible, and persisting until we made it. Don't get me wrong, I wouldn't turn down a million dollar check or salary, but it honestly hasn't been necessary thus far to make our dreams become our reality. It has merely taken living everything I outlined in the first book: positive thinking, drive, and follow through.

Why am I mentioning all of this? Because when I wrote *Z&TOADG*, I had no idea that the book would take off the way it did. On the day of its release, my wife asked me how many copies I thought I would sell, and I responded "I don't know, I'd be happy if I sold 10!" Today, the book has sold thousands of copies worldwide and has been a catalyst for achieving more than I could ever have dreamed possible. Most of that is because of the fans and readers like you. The other part of it is that I fully and passionately believe the philosophies that I outlined in the text of the first book, and I credit those philosophies (and of course, you) for the book's success as well as my own.

Zen & The Art Of Disc Golf was (and continues to be) 100% self published and self promoted, and so will *Discs & Zen*. I am not backed by any disc golf company or big book publisher, and I am not a professional disc golfer (I didn't even stay at Holiday Inn Express last night). I do this for one reason: I love it.

Very shortly after the release of *Z&TAODG*, I was inundated by requests for a follow up book. That simply blew my mind. How does a person write one book about disc golf much less multiple books? That was 20,000 Facebook fans and 11,000 Instagram fans ago. (Okay, so I'm not at @discgolfshoutout's status yet, but there's no need to compare.) Over time, I began being asked more often for new advice on throwing or life, personal questions, and continued to be asked even more often for another book. The Zen Disc Golf Podcast was created, and 30 episodes were recorded which now could be considered 30 hours of brainstorming with Chris Bawden and Tim Steward about what could possibly be covered in a second book. You are reading the product of those requests, questions, podcasts, interviews, and, more generally, my never ending thought train. I supposed that I need to practice more seated meditation.

Since the release of *Z&TAODG*, so many things have changed. Disc golf has continued to teach me more about living the good life. Some lessons were learned on the disc golf course, some through the many amazing people I have met because of the book and podcast, some from the birth of my son, and many revelations have come from just walking around my property visualizing new fairways. In my first book, I outlined how if you are able to pay attention and really take charge of the moment, a round of disc golf can teach you more about yourself and life than most self-help books you will find on the shelf, including this one. But don't put this book down yet! Most revelations on how life should be and how to make things happen already live within you, it just takes relating them to something you are passionate about to bring them out and make them easier to understand. Jesus, Buddha, Krishna, and Lao Tzu were all masters of the metaphor and helping people discover the truths they have already known.

With an open mind and heart, the world becomes your guru. You are in fact reading this book right now because the universe has put it in your hand. In some way, shape or form, you asked for it either by clicking the checkout button on Amazon (thank you), or maybe by swiping your library card (I know there's a copy of the last book somewhere in a library in Sweden), or maybe someone special saw something in their copy, thought of you, and placed it in your hands. Somehow, this book found you, and I am glad.

This book is similar to the first in that disc golf is an anchor point for me to relay pieces of wisdom I have found helpful in creating the life that I want. Looking out my kitchen window at hole number on my own personal heaven, I can assure you these methods work. In this book, I have worked to compile more information that I believe could be of value to you personally and to your game. If you have been a zendiscgolf.com blog subscriber, you may find that I have included many articles from the blog in this book. If you are a podcast listener, you may recognize some of the topics from our Discs & Zen segment within the podcast.

A book publisher I met at a friend's wedding once told me people don't buy cookbooks for the individual recipes, they buy them to have the collection. Well, that is what this book is: a collection of recipes and disc golf related anecdotes that I firstly hope make you think and secondly hope have some spillover into you becoming a great disc golfer and a more successful person. Look, I am not Paul

McBeth or Ken Climo, and I would never claim to be the best disc golfer in the world. I miss putts, I hit trees and lose discs, and though I have aspirations to be a writer, I have no inclination to become a professional disc golfer. I am just a simple guy who loves disc golf and chose to scream it from a mountaintop via ink on paper. In doing so I have lived my own philosophies and created a reality centered on this wonderful game. I now literally live on my own disc golf course because I had one idea (a basket), I decided to make it happen standing in the place I was (my teepad), and I followed through stroke after stroke until I reached my goal (you get the point). You can do all of this too.

With that being said, lets get this thing started!

THE TAO TE "CHING"

"Profound words are not clever.
Clever words are not profound."

- Lao Tzu - *Tao Te Ching*

The *Tao Te Ching* is an ancient Chinese text traditionally attributed to the Chinese philosopher and writer, Lao Tzu (sometimes seen in text as Laozi). The work is a poetic masterpiece and sits permanently on a table in my office so that I may easily access it to reflect on its passages. The simplicity of Lao Tzu's statements in regards to life, paradox, wisdom, illusion, and reality were deeply ingrained in *Zen & the Art of Disc Golf* and in this book, *Discs & Zen*.

The title, *Tao Te Ching,* has been translated many times over, probably without a proper English equivalent. Broken down, *Tao* literally means "way" or "the way." *Te* can be translated to respresent "virtue, strength, character, or even integrity." You will find many instances and reflections of *Te* throughout this book. *Ching* can be defined as "a cannon, a classic, or a great book." Put it together and the *Tao Te Ching* could have easily been called "The Book of the Way of Virtue."

Albert Einstein once stated: "If you can't explain it simply, you don't understand it well enough." Lao Tzu was able to put extremely complex ideas above life into simple stanzas and sections that have stood the test of time, proving that he knew what he was writing about.

After each chapter in this book, you will find a "poetic summary" of what you just read, and in keeping with the idea of the merging of philosophy and disc golf, I have (probably not so cleverly) titled the summaries the *Tao Te "Ching"* as a homage to the beauty of Lao Tzu's 6th century BC work and also in reference to the beautiful sound made by the chains on a disc golf basket. In these summaries I have tried to pull out important ideas from the chapter to help make them more memorable. I do this with the utmost respect to the classic text, consulting it often, in order to brainstorm on the idea of profound simplicity.

CHAPTER 1
HANGING LOOSE

"There is a marvelous inner world that exists within us, and the revelation of such a world enables us to do, to attain, and to achieve anything we desire within the bounds or limits of Nature."

-Raymond Holliwell - *Working with the Law*

My son, Bryce, was born July 30th, 2015, and like most parents, I will never forget the first moment I held him in my arms. He opened his little eyes, and we looked at one another for the first time, sharing a moment that I would never trade for anything in the world. Then, he raised one eyebrow and gave me one of my own contemplative looks as to say, "What are you looking at?" I chuckled to his mother, "I can't deny this one. He's definitely mine!"

Bryce, who was named after Bryce Canyon in Utah, came into this world about nine months after the release of the first book. (It really was a coincidence.) He was a planned surprise, meaning my wife and I knew we were ready to have a child but wanted it to happen naturally without forcing the issue. We decided that we would let it happen when it happened and let the universe and God decide when we were truly ready.

The funny thing about having children is you are never really ready. One of my favorite quotes of all time is when John Lennon said, "Life is what happens when you are busy making other plans." Ironically, this quote is a lyric from one of Lennon's songs called *Beautiful Boy (Darling Boy)*, which he wrote for his son, Sean. It is so true; some things you just can't prepare for. When life changes abruptly, you either change abruptly with it or suffer as you attempt to swim against the current of the universe. Whenever I experience an unexpected life change, after first taking a breath, I tend to ask myself what I can learn from it. Bryce was no exception.

Working 24-hour shifts with the fire department allowed me to have 20 days off a month and many of those days, in the past, were filled with alone time while my wife worked at her job. I have always had ample free time. In the past, during my free time, I was able to play disc golf almost every day and even take the time to write a book about it, but when Bryce came into this world - BOOM - my life seemed to come to a screeching halt. Everything revolved around this tiny life that I now had to help feed, change, and protect. Obviously, I was not alone in this endeavor. Chris, my wife, is an amazing caretaker and makes the job look effortless. For me, however, it did not always come so easily. It is hard to let go of an ample me-time routine that I worked so many years to perfect.

At first, I did what most new parents try to do in this situation. I did not shrink my to-do list. I merely added Bryce to the list, which was already packed with work, play, podcasting, emailing, tweeting, Instagramming, YouTubing, and now fathering, diaper changing, feeding, etc. Talking with a lot of parents, I realize this is initially a normal thing new parents try to do, and it is also exhausting. I don't know at what point the realization occurred, but when it hit me, it hit me hard. I had piled so much onto my plate that I had not even taken a moment to breathe, much less find any sort of mindful practice in months. Here I was, the Zen Disc Golf guy, touting the benefits of breathing, yoga, and disc golf on the Zen Disc Golf Podcast, and not finding my own time to do any of the above for myself. It was unhealthy, and it certainly was not Bryce's fault.

Bryce's expectations of me are to love him, care for him, hold him, and protect him. He didn't care how many podcasts I cut in a month, how many emails I could send in a day, or what my Twitter follower-to-following ratio was.

Those were all expectations I placed on myself, and if I was going to keep up with my own expectations, then the expectations themselves had to change. It was those expectations that were stressing me out, keeping me up at night and making my shoulders and neck stiff. The point is this: life changes, and many times just shuffling those changes into your current routines and attitudes is not enough and may not even be possible. You must constantly look at your own personal priorities and make room for what really matters in life. Being a good father is much more important to me than my Twitter following ratio. Relaxing into fatherhood instead of stressing out about it has, hands down, improved both my personal health and home life.

In addition to disc golf (and yes, I will be getting to some disc talk in a moment), my wife and I enjoy kayaking. Just after we got married, we bought each other used kayaks as wedding gifts. She had kayaked several times before, but I had never been in a kayak. I had wanted to get into kayaking for some time. So as soon as we were able, we put our new kayaks into the truck and headed out to Back Bay in Virginia Beach. We unloaded them at the boat launch, and my wife showed me on dry land how to get the foot pegs set for my height, how to sit in the kayak, how to properly paddle, and also advised me on what to do if the kayak should tip over and send me swimming. The Alpha Male in me was just ready to get into the water and start paddling away, as I have always been a "wing it" kind of guy. We placed the kayaks on the launch, I got inside mine, and I pushed off out into Back Bay. Immediately, I found my kayak to be way less stable than I ever thought it would be. I didn't tip over, but my concern about tipping over into cottonmouth territory stiffened all my muscles up so much that I nearly went into panic mode. I could not paddle, I could not steer, and I knew that I was going to splash into the dirty snake water. "How do people do this?" I wondered. Clearly, this was not the fun that I thought it would be. I wanted out, but I couldn't share that with Chris, who was super relaxed and paddling away, in love with her new kayak. Then, as if I was not stressed out enough, bees started coming out of my boat, stinging me in my legs. We bought our kayaks off a guy from Craigslist who had them stored outside for a long period time, and apparently, bees had made a nest in the foot of my kayak. After teetering on full on panic mode, I made it back to the dock, bees still in my boat, never wanting to kayak again. We loaded up the boats, took them home, I got rid of the bees nest, and I swore that was it. Never again.

A couple of weeks later, after the negative experience wore slightly off, my brother-in-law asked if he could come over and kayak with me while my wife was at work. He had never done it before, but he wanted to try to kayak out in the Chesapeake Bay. Again, the Alpha Male came out of me, and I was down to prove that I could do this, without fear. Things were different now because even though I had only done this once (and horribly at that), this time I was the teacher, and he was the student. I showed him the same things my wife had shown me, acting like a kayaking pro. We went out to the beach and launched into some light surf, and while I made it through the foot tall waves, he immediately tipped over and went straight into the water close to the shore. "Oh no!" I thought, obviously I was not the one to teach anyone how to do this, but he quickly popped his head up, laughed, and jumped back into the boat and pushed off again without a problem.

Watching him initially struggle but persevere took my mind off what I was doing, which was floating along without any problems. Once I realized that, I leaned far left and to my surprise I didn't fall in. Then, I leaned hard to my right, and again to my surprise, I did not fall in. I relaxed in the middle, and I realized that the more I relaxed into it, the better I felt. I wasn't going to tip over. I wasn't going to fall in. I was reminded of the surfing lessons I took on my recent honeymoon in Hawaii (once again not the greatest of successes, but an experience nonetheless). The surf instructor would remind us to always "hang loose" and give the Hawaiian Shaka hand gesture. Until that moment in my kayak, the concept of the importance "hanging loose" was still foreign to me, but now I felt like I finally understood it, and I have seen the principle again and again in many other aspects in life.

The more you stress about possible failure, the more potential you have to fail. Sometimes, you just have to relax into the moment in order to succeed. Put simply, worrying is wishing for something that you don't want to happen. Where you place your mental energy is where your reality will follow.

So, back to Bryce (Then I know you want to talk some disc golf - it's on the way, trust me!). It took me a few months to realize after Bryce was born that I was living my life like the first time I had kayaked. I was tense, stressed out, and trying to make everything work without taking a breath or trying to hang loose. Once I came to the realization that it was no different than paddling a small boat, I relaxed into fatherhood, and the entire family is better for it. When you first become a parent, the baby becomes the guru and smacks you in the face saying "Slow down! You move at my pace now!"

Bryce, kayaking, and surfing ironically have taught me an immeasurable life lesson. That relaxing into something or "hanging loose" is of much greater value than rushing into things, stressing and worrying about things, or being too rigid in my attitudes or routines.

As you might imagine this is where disc golf comes in. In disc golf, the importance of "Hanging Loose," is also immeasurable. Rushing shots is never the best way to increase power or accuracy. Stressing yourself out during a round doesn't make the game more enjoyable or you a better player. And being too rigid in your gameplay will never help you to become a well-rounded player with the ability to see the shots you want to make.

Have you ever rushed a shot, had it go bad, then had to tell yourself to slow down? A rushed shot is almost always a bad one. It is a great way to grip lock and send your disc flying into the fairway on the hole next to the one you're playing. Disc golf should be fun and relaxing. The disc golf course is a place you should never feel rushed.

It is true, some people perform well under pressure, but being utterly stressed out while playing disc golf will never reduce strokes. You won't be able to get your mind in the right place to make good decisions, and if your mental game is not all there, then your physical one will never catch up. It is like when fitness trainers say, "You can't outwork a bad diet." You can't out throw a poor decision.

Disc golf is a sport based on flexibility of play. You must be able to be in the moment and be able to think outside of the box. That is why rigidity has no place on the disc golf course. The game changes too often to believe the same old tricks will always get you wins. The wind changes, the temperature changes, even the course even changes from season to season. You have to be flexible to able to play well.

The best players know that to be a great disc golfer, you have to be able to hang loose, relax, and be in the moment. That is where wins are made, and that is where the fun is to be had.

TAO TE "CHING!"
SLOW DOWN

The faster you go
The more the beauty blurs around you
The faster you throw
The more you sacrifice control

The faster you go
The more you chains you miss
The faster you throw
The more trees get hit

When you slow down
Everything becomes the teacher
Every detail becomes clear
And you become the student
Being taught by the entire Universe

CHAPTER 2
BECOMING LIKE THE CHILD

"The secret of genius is to carry the spirit of the child into old age."

-Aldous Huxley

There are few things in life more remarkable than watching a growing baby discovering and learning about the world around them. They become easily hypnotized and find limitless joy with the things you and I might take for granted on a daily basis. For example, If I hand my son a brand new plastic dump truck complete with working truck bed, LED lights, and buttons that play real truck sounds, he will look at it for about two minutes before his attention has died and the truck has joined the other legions of misfit toys now buried at the bottom of his toy box. Now, If I hand him an old plastic spatula, the child acts like it is Christmas morning, and will entertain himself with it for hours. #dontbuytoys.

Babies and toddlers tend to get excited about the weirdest and wildest things. I personally am mesmerized by watching my son discover something he has never encountered before. For instance, this very morning, I handed my son a single hash brown at breakfast. He slowly reached for it, grabbed it from my hand even slower, and just held it, looking at it for minutes before he ever even thought about eating it. Even after he decided to eat it, he didn't shove the whole thing in his mouth, he deliberately deconstructed it, feeling it with his little hands. Then, smelled it and placed small pieces on his tongue where they no doubt dissolved before he could chew on it. If you and I were to eat each bite like this, we'd never stop eating. All three daily meals would last four hours a piece, and we would never finish one before moving to the next. The point is that children constantly use all of their senses to explore the world on a scale you and I can't even conceptualize. They are the ultimate mindful beings. They are little Buddhas in onesies.

This is how Bryce lives, though. Everything he encounters is a timeless journey into discovery and wonder. I suppose that all little things become big things to little people. Imagine if we, as adults, lived like this, jumping from one intense experience to the next simply because we are taking the time to actually experience it. I am reminded of a Bible verse, Matthew 18:3, "Truly I tell you, unless you change and become like little children, you will never enter the Kingdom of Heaven." To put it another way, to experience the world like a child is to experience the joys of heaven. Children experience the world mindfully and deliberately. They are little explorers without any concept of negativity or danger.

Now obviously, having some inclination of danger protects us as adults. We long ago learned the stove is hot and we probably shouldn't touch it. We also, unfortunately, have learned along the way not all strangers can be trusted,   probably a good thing. We also know which senses are appropriate in discovering new things. We probably have an idea of what a stick tastes like (not good), so we don't need to try tasting another. We know what happens when we try to pet a cactus (ouch), don't need to do that again. We know what the cat box smells like when we hover over it and take a huge whiff (let's avoid that). Our senses have worked with our brains to wire together pathways that allow us to take these shortcuts. The shortcuts listed above are probably good ones to keep using.

But, over time we have developed other sensory shortcuts that may not be improving our lives, and in fact, if we were to eliminate them, everyday stress would not be one of the greatest killers at large. We, as a culture, have become obsessed with being busy. We wear it like a badge of honor sometimes, even bragging to other people how busy we are as if running around like chickens with our heads cut off somehow shows the world how successful we have become. And we make excuses why we can't enjoy ourselves and do the things that we love, or keep ourselves fit and healthy, or help us to grow strong bonds with our family simply because we are too busy (and no-one else really understands).

The old cliche is we probably need to stop and smell the roses. But why? We know what a rose smells like, right? Why take time from our busy lives to stop and experience something already in our memory banks? The answer is this: because it reminds us we are all here. We are living and breathing creatures, and today is all we really have. Yesterday is gone and tomorrow is nothing but swirling fiction in our minds (until it happens, and guess what, when it happens it is today again and not tomorrow).

After spending many hours watching Bryce interact with the world, I have been working to teach myself to slow down and not let "experience shortcuts" become my life. When I am on the course and I pull out that beautiful hunk of plastic joy, I try to take time to look it over and notice both its manufactured beauty (and mentally try to show some appreciation to its crafters) and also notice any flaws caused by the past 20 to 30 trees I've flung it at. I feel the disc in my hand, noticing its weight, grip, and flexibility. Then I chuck that thing as far as I can, hoping to catch a few seconds glimpse of a beautiful flight as the disc soars, glides, and gentle lands mere feet from the basket (so, not every time, but this is my daydream). Then, as I walk down the fairway to my disc, I try to notice everything I can, the smell of freshly fallen pine needles, the crunch of sticks under my feet, the sounds of birds flying overhead and insects in the woods. I try to allow each sense to have a field day to really bring me into the moment. I think of Bryce and try to experience each detail as he would, without putting anything on the course in my mouth. I try to become the child so that I may enter the Kingdom of Heaven on the DGC.

TAO TE "CHING!"
EXPERIENCE THE MOMENT

Take a moment
To experience every sense
Every joy
Once forgotten

The smells of the seasons
The taste of your food
The feeling of a cool wind on your cheek
The beautiful flight of a single plastic disc

The sound of chains ring
Like Tibetan singing bowls
Echoing through the woods
This is heaven

CHAPTER 3
A GAME OF LOSING CONTROL

"The problem is this: man is a self-conscious and therefore self controlling organism, but how is he to control
the aspect of himself which does the controlling?"

-Alan Watts - *This Is It*

I will admit to you that I have a fear of flying. It's not a
debilitating fear, I still get on airplanes and maintain my
composure without having any type of chemical sub-
stance to help. But, when that airplane pulls out onto the
runway and those engines begin to rev up, I really begin
to feel the fear. How I am able to get through this, I suppose, is by reminding myself that the wonderful destina-
tion I am about to journey to is worth letting go of my irrational fear of flying.

Interestingly enough, I have no fear of heights, and I
think I really have less of a fear of death than most people

(as a firefighter, I believe that I face death somewhat more often than most). I also have no fear of riding in cars on the freeway and statistically you have a better chance of dying in a car accident than in an airplane crash. So, I will take my admission one step further and state that my fear of flying is not necessarily a fear of being up in the air or dying in an airplane, it is a fear of not being in control.

I think for many people this fear comes as standard operating software. It may manifest itself in a multitude of different ways including phobias, personality disorders, and utterly strange behaviors. We all have our different ways of handling this fear, but the truth is we all have it. People do not like to give up control.

Now, it is interesting to ask the question: Do we really have total control of ourselves? Obviously, most of us believe we can control our behaviors and our actions, but where do our actions truly begin? They begin with our thoughts and our feelings. In this way, controlling yourself begins with the controlling of our thoughts and our feelings.

Disc golf can become a window to ourselves and to our lives if we are able to step back and ask questions like this. When we step up on the tee pad, we have control over the type of throw we are going use (hyzer, anhyzer, forehand, backhand), our disc selection (Should I throw that old Leopard or try out that new Ibex?), and we have control of our thinking while X-stepping up the tee pad. However, it should be noted that disc selection and shot selection are infinitely easier than controlling our emotional reactions such as anger, anxiety, or lack of self-confidence during the last few seconds of your X-step. But think about this: all control ends when that disc leaves your hand. The flight of that disc and the lie of that disc is dependent on a multitude of factors from the wind, the trees, and the terrain, but the fact remains: once that disc leaves your hands all control is lost.

Now this might sound like I am stating the insanely obvious: to throw something you must let it go. Straight forward right? But it is really worth taking a few seconds to meditate on this idea. Disc golf, as in most sports, depend on letting go and losing control for a few minutes. And losing control means things are not always going to go 100% to plan. In fact, they usually don't. Sometimes you luck out and get yourself a better lie than you considered before stepping up to throw, and sometimes you grip lock and send your disc sailing hard to the right, past 80 trees, and into the middle of the street and hit an old lady's car who is just trying to drive through the park (not that this has ever happened). My point is: the whole game is preparing your best, practicing hours on end, getting your head on straight, and finally letting go of control. The game of disc golf is to let go and move forward.

Again, simple enough concept, right? You pull back, release, and move forward. You may have good lies, you
may have bad ones, but at least you are moving forward.
One statement people who play disc golf with me hear
me say a lot is: "You can see it (the basket) from there."
It's meant as a joke when someone has a poor lie, but it's
true - you got closer to your goal, and you can still see the
basket. It may not have been an ace or a birdie, and it
might sound a little overboard on the positive thinking
boat, but seriously - if you are moving forward and having fun, does it matter?

"You can still see it from there."

Really successful disc golfers know this even if they have
never really labeled it in this way. They know upon release they have done everything that they could do to
control the shot, but once they let go all control is lost.
The only control you have over your round begins in your
head is transmitted through your body, to your hand, and
ends when that plastic leaves your hand. In this way, every shot in our game is a combination of gaining and losing control - over and over again.

In life, it is the same. Truly successful people understand
that success comes with risk, and to never do anything

that scares us or makes us feel like we are not in control would lead to never being able to truly become successful. Success begins with gaining control over yourself and your thinking, followed by releasing control, letting go, and putting yourself out there to win.

Every blog, every podcast, every tweet, and especially every book I write is a combination of controlling content - then releasing it to the world and hoping it flies the way I hope it will. But if I never let it go and set it free to be loved or criticized, it would never have a chance to bring value to myself or others.

In *Z&TAODG*, I coined a simple phrase and printed it largely on the back cover of the book: "Most Importantly, Just Throw." Until now, I have never really delved into attempting to describe what I mean when I say this, mostly because I want it to mean what you need it to mean, whatever meaning you need to derive from it in the moment that you are in.

In some instances, it could mean simply - Just get out and play! Stop reading about it, stop dreaming about it, stop listening to us talk about it on the podcast. Just get out there and play!

In other instances, when used on the course, the phrase "Just throw," could have a more meditative meaning, such as forget everything else and focus on throwing. Drop your baggage, quiet your inner critic, visualize your shot, and simply pull back and release.

The meaning I want to attach to it for the purposes of this chapter is we could rephrase "Just throw" with "Just let go." To some this may sound cliche, to others profound, to me sometimes the most profound concepts are found in the simplest ideas. You can't play disc golf without throwing or without letting go.

I have met so many disc golfers over the past two years who have let go of their fear of being out of control of something and have become really successful as a result. Allow me to list a few:

Chris Bawden and his partner in crime, Rodney Lane, decided to start a blog devoted to reviewing disc golf putters (www.dgputtheads.com). They had no idea, that within a relatively short time this small step would eventually lead to taking over the Zen Disc Golf Podcast and hosting the newly renamed pod, The Just Throw Podcast, where they enjoy thousands of monthly listeners who look to them for all sorts of disc golf advice. They could have rationalized that there are so many other disc golf blogs, why start another?

When the one and only Steve Dodge was looking for

tournament sponsorships from manufacturers in his area, he had been turned down by 23 companies before heading to Vibram. Without fear, Steve set foot in the Vibram offices all set to give a speech to 15 businessmen. Before Steve could complete his speech, the company not only approved sponsoring his tournaments but began talking about teaming up with him to manufacture disc golf discs. Steve was not concerned about 23 rejections, he was concerned with knowing what he wanted even if it meant giving up control. He could have given up and rationalized, if 23 companies have rejected me, Vibram would probably just be the 24th.

Last but not least, one of our favorite interviews on the podcast was David Tucker who runs the youtube channel "Tuck4s1" and the Facebook group "Big Daddy Disc Golf." David, who has character for days, decided he wanted to give back to the disc golf community for all that it has given to him. In video after video, he puts himself out there in order to help people who have challenges with weight or other physical and mental obstacles that disc golf can assist with. David could have rationalized that his input to the disc golf community would not have been of any value. To his many followers, that rationalization would have been simply wrong.

All three of these gentlemen could have kept their ideas to themselves for fear of failure or not being able to control the thoughts of others, but disc golf is a better sport because they exist.

What are you holding onto that letting go of may benefit yourself and others and what is the root of the fear for not letting it loose upon the world? I challenge you to search yourself and try planting the seed of an idea you have had. Start a blog or a youtube channel. Go to that company and ask them to sponsor your disc golf club's event. Write a book! Everyone has talents that make the world a better place and those talents aren't meant to be hidden. Lose the fear and lose control!

TAO TE "CHING!"
JUST LET GO

Over throwing leads to more putts
Over powering leads you out of bounds
Over stepping leads to foot faults
Over thinking leads everything astray

The natural person
Lives in the moment
And gives each moment exactly what the moment de-
serves

By throwing you are letting go
Only by letting go
Do you reach the basket

CHAPTER 4
MAKING ROOM FOR THE USEFUL

"When I let go of what I am,
I become what I might be."

-Lao Tzu

In *Zen & the Art of Disc Golf*, I talked at great length about how your disc golf bag can be seen as a metaphor for all the baggage that you carry around with you from day to day, and how if you do not place your bag on the ground to throw ("dropping your baggage") you severely decrease your accuracy and ability to achieve your goals.

In this chapter, I would like to talk to you about what we place in our bags and how we hold onto discs and equipment that serve no other purpose except to "fill out our bags." It's very interesting to meet and talk to so many new players who begin playing disc golf, starting with very similar disc golf related habits. I believe a psychologist could make a reasonable study of just disc golfers and have the ability to extrapolate trends in human behavior. We often talk about how newer players tend to buy high-speed drivers in hopes that the numbers on the discs alone will put their tee shots where they want them, in the middle of the fairway, with little attention being paid to throwing technique. Another habit or trait that many disc golfers begin with is becoming a disc golf pack rat, or maybe a "bag rat" would be a better term.

A new player will typically begin their disc golf equipment purchasing with one to three discs. In their minds, this is not enough to buy a huge bag and fill it out with unnecessary equipment. As a matter of fact, a newer player may look at other "big bag disc golfers" and scoff to themselves, seeing no point in carrying so many discs. Then, this same player tries out one or two of their friend's discs, has a couple of good shots with said discs, and again mistakes a couple of good throws for good discs. Now, seeing that those discs helped their round so much, they decide they need to acquire those particular discs. They head to the pro-shop to buy them, and while purchasing those, they add maybe one or two more new ones to the stack while they are there. Now they have six or seven discs. He or she can't carry that many discs comfortably in their hands, so they head back to the sporting goods store for a new bag. While trying out different bags, they may rationalize that they should go ahead and buy a bag that they can grow into. So, they buy a disc bag capable of carrying 10-12 discs with enough pockets and pouches to carry their water bottle, score card, keys, phone, sunflower seeds, and pet rabbit. As they head to the counter, they pick up one or two more discs, because you can't enter a pro-shop and not leave without new plastic. Now, they own a 12 disc bag and eight or nine discs that are banging around in the bag (not to mention knocking against their pet rabbit) when they walk on the course. So the logical thing to do is head back to the store and buy a few more discs to fill out the bag. Before they know it, they have bought enough discs to fill a bag instead of ones they actually plan to throw. They continue to throw just a few of the discs from their bag but continue to drag a plethora of extra weight from hole to hole on the course. Extra weight is great for burning calories, and looking cool, but bears no correlation to how well you play. In fact, by the 18th hole, you might be 20-25% more tired from bearing all that extra weight you never used during your game. The good news is that great companies out there have recognized the needs of the disc golfing masses and have created many excellent (though pricey) disc golf bag carts that can help bear the weight. I personally am waiting for Polaris to design a new ATV disc golf saddle bag.

Now, there is nothing wrong with carrying a full bag of discs, though many arguments could be made why you should leave your pet rabbit at home. There are two schools of thought when it comes to how many discs you need to play disc golf. The first school is learn how to shot shape a few staple discs and the second is have a disc for every job and to know those discs like the back of your hand. Neither is wrong, but speaking purely metaphorically how often do we carry unnecessary discs that don't serve our game and are mainly souvenirs from our local disc golf pro-shop? And using this concept as a metaphor for our emotions and behaviors, how often do we carry negative thoughts, feelings, and emotions around with us on a daily basis that don't serve us in the game of life, and wear them as if they are badges of experience.

Every "negative" emotion we have such as anger, fear, and anxiety, has evolved within the human experience to some extent as a way to aid us in recognizing imminent threats or bodily harm. Emotions generally remove the concept of rationality in attempt to simplify our mental processes and get us out of harm's way. In other words, if we had to constantly scan and rationalize every experience we have as being helpful or harmful, it would be simply be too exhausting to survive. So, emotions take away some of that mental processing and put our bodies in states that allow us to survive without constantly scanning whether or not an experience is good or bad. Emotions take on some of the work, and they help prior experiences stick in memory, so if we have a similar experience in the future, we may begin to feel what we felt during a past harmful experience without the brain having to work to rationalize that this might be an entirely new experience.

For example, one major feeling or emotion that I want to touch on is worry. The feeling of worry exists purely to help us prepare for bad things, but unfortunately for many of us today, there is always something to worry about. Often, we make preparations to discontinue that worry, but we immediately find something else over which to worry. This creates emotional burnout where we simply stop preparing and start to just worry endlessly. Your worry is the most profitable emotion in our current economy. Just ask the news media, advertisers, banks, insurance companies, etc. They can always sell you something to ease your worry while inventing something else for you to worry about and another product to sell. Worry is generally experienced in much longer periods than some other emotions and as a result, loses much of its rationality because it doesn't serve to protect us against some imminent harm. And, isn't it true that most of the things we worry deeply over never occur the way we worried they might?

Beyond making sure we are prepared for possible harm, constant worry is negative visualization. It is praying for what you don't want to happen.

So, if you step up on the tee box and worry about hitting that tree you seem to always hit, you may just hit that tree. Especially, if you announce to your group that you probably will hit that tree because now you have made a verbal plan to hit that tree.

If you refuse to play in the tournament that you have been thinking about playing, because you are worried about how you will feel when you hit the usual tree with everyone looking, you need to understand that the worry you feel in that moment is visualization of that experience happening and because your brain can't tell little difference between reality and your visualization of reality, the worry that you feel is just as bad as the possible embarrassment you think you might feel. The worst part is you never even had to hit the tree in a real tournament to feel that embarrassment. In other words, the worry is worse than the embarrassment!

Some people wear their negative emotions and feelings as a badge, like a souvenir for their misgivings. In the case of worry, some people like to reframe their worry to others as caring for them. For example, they worry about you and call it caring about you. But constantly worrying about other people only serves to exclusively see bad outcomes for other people. Now, I ask you, is constantly visualizing bad outcomes for other people really caring for them or is it discouraging them from reaching for their goals?

Some people wear the badge of anger and carry it as a souvenir for their misgivings and bad experiences. They will qualify it as a means of self-protection, but really it only harms them by not letting the good that life has to offer in. It often keeps the good away: good feelings, good experiences, good emotions, and even good people. They may think it is a means protection, but really, to the outside world, it is victimization. Believing they have something to always be angry about makes the assumption that they will forever be a victim.

Some people carry around the badge of sadness, as a souvenir for their misgivings and bad experiences. These people have resolved to never be happy because the world is a cruel and awful place. What they really want is for someone to feel sorry for them. Asking another person to feel bad with you is one of the most selfish things you could ever ask for.

Once again, emotions have their place. They warn us of imminent danger or threat, but once the danger or threat is removed, they are to be recovered from. Holding onto emotions past the point of recovery is similar to hanging onto discs that you don't need to carry because they "fill out your bag." Every once in a while, you should open up your disc golf bag and see what extra weight you are carrying and remove it. Do this like you are weeding a garden. Still can't throw that Nuke, Viper, or Spirit? Why weigh yourself down with discs you don't need? Create room in your bag for an extra Valkyrie, Stalker, or Lace.

This is not to underestimate the tragedies that people find themselves in from time to time. As I mentioned above, emotions help us deal with negative situations that are oftentimes not preventable, however humans were not designed to live with long-term sustained negative thoughts, feelings, and emotions. When we sustain these feelings it actually does physical harm to our bodies, it makes us ill, and as I mentioned above, it keeps the good stuff away.

Disc golf has helped lead thousands of people through bad times as a way to reflect and find focus in a world where sometimes coping takes all the energy you can muster, but for many this may not be enough. Sometimes we need help in order to become the best possible versions of ourselves. We need mentors and coaches who we can return to in order to help us progress and move forward in life. For some people, that might be friends or family, and for others, doctors and counselors. The first step is recognizing that you are carrying a badge or souvenir of negativity from long ago, and that life would be much better if you were somehow able to just let go.

Just because you were handed a bunch of negativity many moons ago doesn't mean you're still required to carry it everywhere you go.

And PS: I really played disc golf with someone who insisted on bringing their pet rabbit in their bag, every round. True story!

WEEDING THE GARDEN

Most traps we find ourselves in
Were set by us in the past
But we hold the key to set ourselves free
Release yourself.

Your negative emotions
Are not trophies
You don't need to carry them
You don't need to show them off

Where worry lives,
There is no room for contentment.
Where anger lives,
There is no room for forgiveness.
Where sadness lives,
There is no room for gratitude.

Where there is no room for gratitude,
There is no room for blessing.

CHAPTER 5
GRATITUDE FUELS ATTITUDE

"Develop an attitude of gratitude, and give thanks for everything that happens to you, knowing that every step forward is a step toward achieving something bigger and better than your current situation."

-Brian Tracy

I was playing a round with a friend of mine the other day who was having a hard time with a couple of holes, and as a result, his score was falling behind. He began complaining about his round and someone in the group laughed, saying to him: "Well, at least you're having fun!" to which he quickly responded "I'm losing. I don't have fun when I lose!"

When you really stop to contemplate this statement, you realize that he is placing an extremely high standard on whether or not he ever has fun playing disc golf at all. That is really a high qualifier to place on your own happiness or level of fun. On that day, there were four of us playing, which meant he had a one-in-four chance of having fun, based on his own personal standard. This doesn't even count all of the other elements outside of his control, wind, weather, course condition, extreme temperature, level of practice, level of energy, ability to focus, lack of mosquitos nipping at you through 18 layers of DEET and Permetherin, all of the elements that help determine whether or not you might win.

This made me ask myself: what is my own personal standard of happiness on the course? I thought about it for a few minutes and came up with this mission statement: My standard for fun on the course is being outside, playing a game I love, possibly with the company of people I enjoy. And because this happens every round, as long as I remember this is my own personal standard, I have a much higher chance of finding enjoyment every time I step onto the course to play.

I will never say winning isn't important, we should strive to win, but our happiness should not be based on a standard left so highly to chance.

In life, we set our own standards and expectations every day. Unfortunately, when we set our standards and expectations too high and base them on factors we can't control, we allow our emotions to be controlled by chance, but if we are able to take a step back and reframe our standards and expectations for happiness, we have a much better chance of becoming consistently content with longer and more frequent periods of true happiness.

You will notice my standard for happiness on the course revolves closely around being grateful. I am grateful for being able to be outdoors, for having good company, for having the time and the good health to play such a truly fun game. Gratitude is the shortest route to happiness and contentment.

We could all use this outlook on life to a greater extent. Look around you right now. Look at all you have: the people, your possessions and your environment. All of these things are the product of the actions you took to get them. Hopefully all of these people and things were what you wanted at some point and because you were driven to get them, you got them. Seriously, look around and notice how everything in your life began with a choice that was followed by an action.

After the release of *Z&TAODG*, I realized (with much regret) that I failed to mention how much gratitude influences attitude, and because attitude is the foundation for everything happening in your life, you must understand the correlation between the two.

Gratitude fuels attitude. When we have a gratitude mind-set, the mind starts looking for ways to fulfill vision. Vision is anything we want: a good drive, sinking a putt, a promotion at work, anything! The opposite of gratitude is thanklessness, and when we are programmed, either by ourselves or our upbringing to only see the things we don't have, things that we can't do, all sorts of negativity, our mind becomes programmed in that direction and where the mind goes, so does the body.

Dissatisfaction occurs when you place too much emphasis on what you don't have or what you can't control. You can change that. You can create your own standard for happiness, contentment, and even what you find fun. It is up to you to find them, reflect on them, and enjoy this life!

A gratitude routine you can use at home that I think is really effective is the Jar Method. Use a jar, box, or container and put it at your front door with small slivers of paper next to it, and every day before you leave your house take one of the sheets of paper and write down the following:

1. Something that you are grateful for.
2. Something that you want.

3. What actions you are taking to get you there.

A disc golf example would be:

1. I am thankful for all of this excellent plastic in my disc golf bag.
2. I would like to sink more 25 foot putts.
3. I am going to do this by practicing putting every day using the (fill in the blank) method.

Another every day example might be:

1. I'm thankful that I wake up every morning with a roof over my head.
2. I would really like a promotion at work.
3. I am going to do this by leading by example and thus showing value to my employer.

On the disc golf course you can also develop a gratitude routine by thinking of something you are thankful for on every tee box. By the end of the round you have expressed gratitude 18 or more times. That is probably 18 more times than most of the people you will run into during the day. Your gratitude will fuel your attitude and people will begin to notice.

Attitudes are contagious (both good and bad). This is such an easy way to influence the world around you with very little energy. Ripples of good energy will become waves and those waves will become tsunamis.

TAO TE "CHING!"
GRATITUDE

Like a parent and a child
The Universe gives you what you need

The grateful child is constantly blessed
The unappreciative child becomes cursed
But when the thankless child finally says "thank you."
He becomes blessed like the grateful child

Who would you reward?
The person who gives you thanks?
Or the one who takes from you without appreciation?

The first step to being blessed further
Is to recognize all of your current blessings

CHAPTER 6
FROM THE DISC'S PERSPECTIVE

"It's so mysterious and so elusive because what you are in your inmost being escapes your examination in rather the same way that you can't look directly into your own eyes without using a mirror, you can't bite your own teeth, you can't taste your own tongue and you can't touch the tip of this finger with the tip of this finger and that's why there's always an element of profound mystery in the problem of who we are."

- Alan Watts

A few weeks ago, I was playing a doubles round at Newport News Disc Golf Course with some friends of mine when I suddenly I had a revelation.

I have recently introduced most of these players to the game, and even though they had played the course several times from the short tees, they had never played from the long tees. I also thought that a doubles round would give them a little more game variation and be a good starting point for them to begin playing a slightly longer course.

We paired stronger players with weaker players to ensure some balance in the game, and everyone was playing extremely well. I fully believe that switching up the tees, baskets, or even the course is a great way to step outside of the box and really see what you can do. For some reason, forcing yourself outside of your routine seems to help you break out of complacency and helps to influence the mindfulness and focus that disc golfers require to play well.

When we stepped onto the long tee on hole number 6, everyone looked stumped. For the first time they encountered a tee box with no real clear line to the basket, just a row of jail bars made up of trees and limbs. I watched as their confidence broke and my friends resigned themselves to double bogeys on the hole before ever driving off the tee. Then, I stepped up to the box and launched a right handed, back-hand throw. The disc threaded through the trees and made a line closing in on the basket. The whole group looked on as if they were going to finally see their first ace in person, and I froze thinking it was about to hit chains. But at the last moment, the disc hit a tree and ricocheted hard left into what appeared to be the thickest part of the woods and almost ended up on the fairway of another hole. Everyone immediately laughed with me as they imagined how bad my current lie must have become after the ricochet.

My partner got ready to step up to the tee box and asked me: "What should I do? Should I play it safe and just try to throw a straight shot and keep it in the open?"

I told him that sounded like a good idea. He stepped up on the box, gave a nice soft toss, and landed the disc in the open about seventy-five feet ahead. The shot was not thrown very far, and there was a long distance to the basket, but it was safe and in the middle of the fairway. Everyone congratulated him on the throw, and the group began to push forward.

"I guess we will be using my shot!" he proudly said, believing he was stating the obvious.

I answered him, "Maybe... Let's see."

He laughed at me, believing I must have been joking. We both walked up to his disc and noticed that while he was in the open, we still had about one hundred feet to go, and in addition, there were trees forming a jail cell around the basket. He got ready to put his mini down when I said,

"Wait a minute, let's see if my lie is any better." He immediately turned to me and chuckled.

"Are you kidding?" he asked while looking at me like I had horns growing out of the sides of my head."

"Just hold on…" I replied, laughing and headed toward my disc that had cut hard left and laid there in what appeared to be the thickest part of the woods. But when I got to my disc, much to my own surprise, I realized that my lie was not bad at all. As a matter of fact, I had a clear shot with about thirty feet to the basket. What I thought was my worst drive ever on this hole turned out to be probably be one of the best. I yelled back, "Let's go with mine!"

Again, my partner swore I had to be joking with him. He headed my way leaving his bag and disc behind, swearing his disc had to have the better line to the basket. When he got to my disc, he looked at the clearing and simply said: "Whoa. Great shot!" He returned to his bag, picked it up, and headed back to my disc in the woods. Together we birdied the hole.

The moral of the story is you can't always judge a shot from the tee box. You must see the shot from your disc's perspective before you can make any judgments about your lie. Some of the worst-looking drives and upshots produce the best looks at the basket, as it is not the flight that makes the game, but the lie. Watching a disc soar through the air is one of the most fun parts of the game, but ultimately it is where the disc lands that matters. In this, I am reminded of a cartoon that shows two versions of success. The first version makes success appear to be a consistent, straight line connecting two dots in an upward motion, and underneath the caption reads, "What people think success looks like." The second version has the caption, "What success really looks like." The line squiggles all over the place, up and down, side to side, and making twisting turns as if my fifteen-month-old son had drawn it with a crayon. The cartoon is showing that success is rarely ever found in one smooth step, but most times appears ugly until the goal is reached. Ask Thomas Edison who reminded the public that he never failed when he created the lightbulb, he "just found ten thousand ways that wouldn't work."

After throwing my disc from the tee and watching its beautiful flight being knocked off its line, I could have gotten mad, kicked my bag, and cursed at the tree for disrupting my flight, but I didn't. I have seen many times in this game what appears to be a bad shot from the box might just become one of the best shots you've ever made. Winning isn't always about relying on your perspective from the tee. It is about taking each shot as it goes and seeing each shot from the disc's perspective.

In life, we believe we make judgments solely based on our five senses: touching, tasting, smelling, hearing, and seeing. Our actual judgments use our sensory input, but then are run through a filter of our experience and programmed beliefs.

Beginning with my senses:
I watched my disc have a beautiful flight.
I saw it hit a tree.

Filtering through my past experiences:
In the past, hitting trees has been bad for my game.

Final judgment:
This shot went bad.
I probably have a bad lie.

While our senses are the only way our brains can receive information from the outside world, our final judgments may not necessarily reflect our actual situation in our lives. With our eyes we may not see clearly. With our ears we may not hear acutely. When my hands are cold I may not be able to feel something perfectly. Our senses are never perfect, yet they form the basis of our understanding of the world. Then they get even more messed up as we filter them through experiences and bogus beliefs that have nothing to do with our current situation. This leads to so many misunderstandings in our lives.

And unfortunately, when we must make a judgment or decision based on imperfect information, it may be clouded and downright irrational.

So what is the solution? One word: *understanding*.

Understanding means knowing that you don't always have perfect information. That none of us are perfect in general. That just because you see something is wrong doesn't mean another person does. Understanding means coming to terms with our own imperfections and the imperfections of those around us by stepping off of our personal tee pads and into the perspective of the disc or of another person. This also means having compassion and forgiveness for ourselves and others.

Do not be so hard on yourself when things don't seem to go your way. When you lock yourself into your own perspective, you may not see how great you are doing, how far you have come, and how close you are to achieving what you want.

It is important to surround yourself with people who are able to provide you with fresh perspectives. I do not mean people who will always praise you or always criticize you. I mean people who are compassionate and have a sincere interest in watching you succeed. In order to do this, they are willing to let you know when you are succeeding and when you are screwing up. For some, this could be a teacher, a mentor, a coach, or even a parent or grandparent. For me, this person is my wife. And just as important as it is to surround yourself with these people, it is even more important to be open to listening to their perspectives on how you are doing.

When I was a young teen someone told me, "It's funny you can never truly see yourself, even the mirror image of you is backwards." This idea has stuck in my head for a long time, and it simply means the only way to gain true perspective is to change your perspective altogether. You must be objective in order to see things as they really are. The actor doesn't know his character as well as the playwright. The model doesn't know his image as well as the painter. The athlete doesn't know his abilities as well as the coach. Because disc golf is a teach-yourself, solitary sport, to get better at it we may need to find a coach or someone who is better than us and has a sincere interest in seeing us become a better players.

Contemplate this: We think we know what we know, but what we know is only what we think we know.

Let me explain a little further, and then we will return to disc golf. For over fifteen years I was an electronic musician and producer. I wrote, recorded, and engineered all of my own work with some help from other musician friends (Begin shameless self-promotion here: I played in many bands, including Media Violence and Aggressive Attack. If you like industrial electronic music I wouldn't be offended if you checked out my old stuff on iTunes. End shameless self-promotion). I was a perfectionist in the studio, wanting to get my mixes perfect, but what I found was the more time I spent alone, perfecting, the more I would screw it all up and have to start all over. The best mixes I did were the ones that I completed quickly and used more intuition than trying to do it by the book. The more I sat there and judged my work, the more I hated it, but if I would take a break from it and give it a couple of days, I could come back fresh and breathe new life into the mix. The only thing more powerful than taking a break from it was to bring in someone else who I trusted to give me an objective opinion. Those two methods combined would help me to produce and mix much better than sitting in a dark room listening to the same four bars of music until they consumed my soul.

The first book, podcast, and blog are sources for many people who want try to improve their disc golf games and lives. Not a week goes by that I don't receive an email from someone wanting to get better at the game who starts off with something like this:

> I just don't get it. I play 36 holes every
> day, but my drives aren't getting any bet-

ter, and recently my putting has been in the toilet. I practice every day, but I just can't get any better. How can I break my slump?

They get really surprised when I respond: "Take a break." First of all, you are probably wearing your body out. Secondly, because your body is tired, you are reinforcing bad habits. And thirdly, you need a change of perspective. When you come back to play, bring someone with you and maybe play a different course altogether. This is exactly like me sitting in the studio tinkering with my songs until I have destroyed them completely.

Becoming a better player means having to occasionally step outside of your routines. To gain true perspective you must change your perspective altogether.

TAO TE "CHING!"
PERSPECTIVE

You cannot witness you
Until you step outside of you
The mirror is of no help
Because it is still you within you
Doing the observation

You must step away from routine
And return to new routine
To see how far you have come

Just as a lobster doesn't feel the heat
Rising as he begins to boil
You cannot sense the harm of habit
Until you remove the habit
And begin to see the change

CHAPTER 7
ON SELF-LIMITING BELIEFS

"You hit what you aim at and if you aim at nothing you will hit it every time."

- Zig Ziglar

I see this next behavior happen very often on the course. I'm out with a buddy who starts a round off playing amazing, birdieing the first couple of holes in a row, and feeling great about it. Then they turn to me and say something close to one of the following:

1. "Man, I'm doing great on the front nine, watch the back nine just destroy me!"
2. "I never play this well, I hope I can keep it up."
3. "Four down on the front 9, that means I have four bogeys waiting for me on the back nine."

Then what happens? They make this statement a reality. They turn around and do exactly what they have said they were going to do: bogeying enough holes on the back nine to even out their score and match their expectations of themselves.

Why does this always seem to happen?

Let me put it simply: You can never win against your own self-limiting beliefs which you hold to be true.

No matter who you are, a brand new player on the course or Paul McBeth, you have an image of yourself within your mind that is so ingrained in your personal beliefs that the laws of the universe serve to prove to you that you *are* who you *think* you are. This belief system can either take you to endless heights or hold you back completely unnecessarily. If you have mentally placed a glass ceiling on your disc golf score, rest assured your attitude, focus, and actions will follow the instructions given to them by your own personal belief system known as your self-image.

And before we move on, let me say that last statement one more time, replacing only a few words: If you have mentally placed a glass ceiling on *anything you want in life*, rest assured your attitude, focus, and actions will follow the instructions given to them by your own personal belief system known as your self-image.

We all step on our favorite courses knowing what we normally shoot. Some players use this as a benchmark to improve. Other players allow it to be the score that defines them. From our earlier example, no matter how well they play on the front half of the course, they will make it up on the back.

Now there are two different ways we mentally encode our self-limiting beliefs:

1 . **Internally** - This is the mode of the pessimist, the player that believes no matter how well they play, some universal power will ultimately destroy it in the end.

2 . **Externally** - This is the mode of the player or person who allows other people to define their self-image. This person then believes and internalizes the vision that other people have of them.

Both ultimately involve your mind encoding and accepting a self-limiting idea as a fact and therefore transferring it into a belief, and making it irrefutable.

Let me give you a personal, real-world example: Twenty years ago, when I was in grade school, I knew what an acceptable report card was to bring home to my parents in order to escape punishment. I knew that I was required to have all As or Bs in all my subjects, but I was allowed to have one C if I had an extra A to balance it out. Guess what every report card I brought home looked like? That's right: two A's, three B's, and one C. Same report card every grading period. Coincidence? Years later, in college, the only expectation I had was to "do my best." There was a reason I was a straight-A college student and somewhat of a slacker high school student. I let someone else set my limitations and I lived up to them.

The message here is that every single one of us has a self-image and every single one of us has, in some way, set fictional limits on our ability to succeed. In order to over-come this, we must discover and weed out those self-lim-iting beliefs and create a self-image that accurately re-flects who we are and what we are capable of becoming. What I would like you to do, is examine your own self-image and figure out what self-limiting beliefs you are holding onto that are holding you back on the course and in your life. It can take a long time to let go of long-held beliefs but the brain was designed to do it. Neurons create associations through webs daily through a process called neuroplasticity. They can also break down old webs that are no longer helpful for your survival. Once you ac-knowledge that this is a fact, you can no longer make the excuse: "I can't help it! It's how I've always been..." You CAN help it. You CAN change your mind about you. Think of your potential if you had the determination to blow past glass ceilings and strive to give your all to your passions. Think collectively about a nation or a world that would commit to not believing that our past failures or events do not anchor our futures. Think about it!

TAO TE "CHING!"
SELF-IMAGE

Every day we draw ourselves
In our minds

Sometimes we make errors
And leave them behind
Sometimes we give the pen away
And ask for someone else to draw
And we become the image they left behind

These pictures become us
But we often forget
We can take control
We can erase
We can re-draw

The drawing should be of who we are
Instead of us becoming the drawing

CHAPTER 8
ON REALISTIC EXPECTATIONS

"The change is from inner to outer…We start by dissolving our attitude not by altering our conditions."

- Bruce Lee - *Striking Thoughts*

I was playing a round with a friend of mine the other day, let's call him Bruce W., simply because I don't really know a Bruce W., so that will help keep his identity anonymous.

Bruce asked me to come play a round with him, telling me that he needed to get out of the house. His wife had begun to really stress the poor guy out with what he referred to as her "relentless nagging."

Bruce met me in the parking lot and after a few practice putts and small talk about the weather and new disc purchases, we headed off to the first tee box. I selected my go-to driver and he selected his. He asked me to lead off the match, and I stepped up and threw about a 300-foot bomb around the first set of trees where it headed straight for the basket before smacking a tree about 25 feet from the chains. Then it caught a bad skip across another fairway and into a ditch filled with just about the brownest, mosquito breeding water you've ever seen. Bruce patted me on the back, saying with a smirk, "Nice shot."

"Thanks," I responded.

Bruce went on, "No, I mean it, that line was perfect and it looked like it was headed straight for chains until that tree grew up from underneath it!"

We both laughed.

Bruce stepped up on the tee box and said he was going to try the same line, minus the tree. He stood on the tee visualizing, a technique I had taught him in earlier rounds. Then he took a slow X-step before sending a rocket straight down the middle of the fairway. The only problem is the middle of the fairway is completely blocked by trees and his disc hit the first tree so hard that for a few milliseconds, I swore he had thrown a hardshell taco instead of a disc.

"Nice shot," I told him, giving him a taste of his own medicine.

He took one look at me through half-slanted eyes and bent over saying nothing. Then he snatched up his bag straps before barreling toward his disc. When he got to his disc he pulled out a putter and attempted to throw a hyzer line back around the trees, when all of the sudden, a bad gust of wind floated it over the fairway and out of bounds. Again he snatched his bag up, saying: "I guess this is just how it's going to be today! Can't do anything right! May as well quit and go home."

I did not respond, leaving him alone for a few minutes and walked over to my disc. I rolled up my sleeves and braved the murky water to retrieved my beloved plastic. Bruce stood at the OB line, took a few seconds, and then completely canned a beautiful 75-foot putt. I threw about two or three more strokes before chaining out when I finally got close enough to the basket, and I marked a 5 on the score card. Bruce was sitting at the tee box on the next hole when I joined him again.

"I'm sorry I acted like that," he said.

"It's OK man…" I began. People seem to think they always have to apologize to me on the course for poor etiquette. I'm not sure why.

"No, really," he responded quickly. "I'm just having a hard time at home is all." He sat on the bench and began explaining all the things at home and work that were stressing him out, and all the reasons he needed to get out and throw a round. "When I threw that awful shot off the tee, I just knew that I had brought all my bad luck out here. Wanted to relax is all. And a terrible first shot wasn't what I was looking for." He said.

"Well, that putt you made was beautiful. Probably one of the best I've ever witnessed." I told him.

"I know, right! I couldn't believe I made it, but I guess after hitting that long putt, I got to thinking about how stupid I was acting on the first part of the hole."

"It's alright man, let's move on! Play the rest of the round off that good feeling!" I stated.

Bruce and I continued down the course. In between shots, Bruce confided in me about his wife. "She is always telling me stuff I need to do! 'Cut the grass! Weed the garden! Clean out the garage! When are you going to paint that window trim?' I can't even sit down for a moment to relax! I was lucky enough that she let me out of the house to come out to play the course! Meanwhile, she just sits there all day. The floors aren't getting swept, dishes aren't getting done, and I can't remember the last time she made a bed! Then she had the nerve to tell me I was driving her crazy and she needed a night out with her girlfriends last night. I almost brought up all the stuff around the house that needed doing, but I decided let her go so I could get some peace and quiet."

I walked with him and listened to his complaints between shots, and when the moment seemed right, I finally had to ask him, "Bruce, when you came out today, did you expect a perfect game?"

"What do you mean?" he asked.

"Did you expect all birdies, maybe even an ace today?"

"No, just expected to come out and play and have a good time. Why? What are you getting at?"

"Well, if you expected to just get out and throw a few and have a good time, why did you get so upset back on hole one when things didn't go as planned?"

"Look, I said I was sorry about that…"

"No, man, still nothing to apologize about. But you talk about having one expectation then get really upset when things aren't perfect." I paused for my shot. "When you get home and you notice that the floors still haven't been swept, what do you do?"

"I calmly ask her if she would sweep the floor."

"And how does she respond?"

"She gets all bent out of shape and starts explaining how I don't understand how hard it is to watch the kids all day and that every time I am seeing her, it's her one moment she has to relax."

"So what I am hearing is that you believe you are being constantly nagged by someone you are constantly nagging?"

"Well, I wouldn't define what I do as nagging."

"Of course you don't. But neither does she. Bottom line is, it sounds like you both need to work out your expectations of one another and communicate them."

"Yeah, we could do better with that I suppose."

We continued playing the round, and Bruce stopped complaining- started playing, having a good time, and beat me in the end. I'm still waiting for my rematch.

The keyword here is expectations. Oftentimes we need to not necessarily lower our expectations but give them some basis in reality. You aren't going to play a perfect round every time you hit the course. And guess what, the people you surround yourself with aren't going to be perfect all the time either. It should be our goal to not only try to become better people every day but to cut people a little slack from time to time. Start with yourself; cut yourself a little slack. You are going to have bad shots, bad rounds, and bad days. You are going to be tired, angry, sad, happy, all within due time - cut yourself some slack. But remember to cut the other people in your life some too, and hopefully when you mess up, your real friends will cut you all the slack you need but no more. Your real friends will step in and let you know where the slack needs to end.

At the end of our round, Bruce shook my hand and told me he appreciated the round and the talk. He even said, "You know, I knew exactly how I was messing up while I was doing it. I just needed you to help me get past myself and say it." Then he looked harshly at me and said, "You're not going to put this in your next book, are you?"

"Not if you don't want me to." I laughed.

Bruce threw his bag in the trunk of his car and said, "Nah, put it in the book. Maybe it will be useful to someone else."

"Okay." I laughed again.

"Just do me a favor, don't use my real name. Call me something cool, like Batman."

"Done."

TAO TE "CHING!"
EXPECTATIONS

The quickest path to misery
Is to paint a perfect mental picture
Hold reality up to it
And decide if the two are not identical
You will never be happy

CHAPTER 9
PRACTICING TO MISS THE CHAINS

"But usually, without being aware of it, we try to change something other than ourselves, we try to order things outside us. But it is impossible to organize things if you, your self are not in order. When you do things in the right way, at the right time, everything else will be organized."

- Shunryu Suzuki - *Zen Mind, Beginners Mind*

Have you ever grabbed a handful of putters and gone out to your favorite practice basket, only to leave putting practice thinking: "I'm not really sure if that session made me a better or worse putter..." Did you start strong and finish weak? I know I have. In fact, I just left the backyard to type this chapter with a similar feeling.

Shouldn't we leave practice feeling like we are stronger players than we started? That *IS* the point of practice, isn't it?

A little while ago, I grabbed a handful of Discmania putters that I'm testing out. I have a few different types of plastics and have been throwing them around the yard, trying to figure out which plastic suits me best.

My backyard practice routine involves me starting approximately eight feet from the basket and moving outward while also changing my angle. The eight-foot mark is a "confidence builder" mark. That is where I start myself out to get a handle on my technique, a feel for my discs, and to hear the chains ring a little bit before I move out further across the yard.

I hit those eight-foot putts – boom, boom, boom, boom.

My next mark is about ten to twelve feet further from the basket, and coming at it from slightly different angle. I hit most of those putts as well – boom, boom, fail, boom.

Then, I'll head out a little bit further to about fifteen to eighteen feet – boom, boom, fail, fail.

I try to overlook the last few failed putts and head out to about twenty to twenty five feet – fail, boom, fail, fail.

Okay, now I'm missing more than I'm hitting, so I start the process over. I head back to my "confidence builder" mark around eight feet from the basket – boom, fail, boom, fail.

Wait a minute... Why am I missing so many eight foot putts now? Eight feet is my confidence builder, not a challenge!

I try again – boom, fail, fail, fail.

Whoa... "What is going on here?" I asked myself. My arm is not tired. The wind hasn't picked up. No one sprayed PAM on my chains while I wasn't looking. Why am I missing?

Then it hit me. When I grab 4 putters and machine gun them at the basket, not taking the time to set up each shot as if it is important, then I am not practicing to make putts, I am practicing to miss them. And my practicing to miss the chains is going great!

Every once and a while, I am reminded that even in practice, it is important not to let your mind slip and go back to what I called in *Z&TAODG*, auto-pilot. If you do not setup in your mind and body that each shot is your first shot, then you are allowing your muscle memory to learn to miss, and by doing this, you are practicing to fail. It is important to focus on making each putt instead of just machine gunning one after another. This is the age old quantity over quality argument. If practice is not quality practice and is merely quantity practice, you may be hurting yourself in the long run through wearing out your body and creating poor habits at the same time. It is especially important to refocus yourself after a missed putt or terrible drive during your field time sessions. If you repeatedly miss a practiced putt and do not "reset" yourself, but rather continued throwing and missing, then you are training your body to miss chains and not hit them.

Leaving practice, you should feel as if you have achieved something. When we practice to miss because we go on auto-pilot for quantity of shots over quality of shots, we leave practice feeling burned. Without correcting that feeling we will carry it with us into the next tournament round.

Catching yourself involves coming off auto-pilot and practicing mindfulness on the course. The next time you find yourself practicing to miss, catch yourself, do a "reset," and remember to practice every shot like it is the only shot you get.

If you feel like your round is slipping, like you're just not hitting putts like you should, or your drives are hitting more cars than fairways, this is the best time to stop everything and takes a few deep breaths. Ask yourself if you went on auto-pilot and if you feel like you did, you need to land that plane before you throw again.

TAO TE "CHING!"
AWARENESS

To live fully
You must be full of life

Life is a string of moments
Awareness of moments
Is awareness of life

Living in a careless daze
You are merely buying your time
And selling it to waste

CHAPTER 10
THE BENEFIT OUTWEIGHS THE EXCUSE

"Bad weather always looks worse through a window."

- Tom Lehrer

Fall is my favorite time of the year. The weather on the East Coast finally seems to be manageable. It is not too hot, not too cold, and I find myself out on the course more, witnessing the leaves changing color and the disc golf course begins to appear like it would be an inspiration for an impressionist painter such as Monet or Renoir. Or a writer like myself.

I have never considered myself a "fair-weather disc golfer." When I was hit by the disc golf fever again a few years ago, I picked up my plastic and I was out at my local course every day. Rain. Snow. Heat. I was more dependable than the United States Post Office (then again, I am not sure how much that is actually saying.) What I mean is: if it was 7am at the Bayville Disc Golf Course in Virginia Beach, Patrick McCormick was throwing on the course.

Some of my friends thought I was insane. We would plan to tee off at 7am and I would end up calling them from the first tee box at 7:15 asking: "Where are you?" and I would hear: "Are you crazy? It's raining!"

I would respond: "Well... Plastic isn't going to melt in the rain, and I have a rain jacket." But that statement was never very convincing to someone still cozy and warm under their covers. So, I played many rounds by myself when the weather conditions were not ideal for most. Ironically, some of these were my favorite and most memorable rounds.

Don't get me wrong, if it was absolutely pouring, I probably would not go out, but you would be amazed what a light sprinkle does to thin out the herd on the course. Playing alone in a light rain can be an amazing event. All is quiet on the course, and listening to the rain hit the leaves on the trees is one of the most relaxing sounds there is. Often in light rain, even when I am not playing disc golf, I will retreat to the woods on my property and just stand there, listening to tiny drops fall through the leaves, and feel them on my face and hands. I have yet to find a mindfulness activity that can bring you more into the moment and appreciate nature being nature.

Similarly, playing in the snow or while it is actually snowing is amazing as well. It adds a whole new element to the game and to the serenity of the course. But you will not find many players out there doing it.

Recently, I took a trip to see five national parks around Utah and Arizona. Of course, the main sight that I wanted to see was the Grand Canyon. It had been a dream of mine as long as I could remember: to sit on the edge of the canyon and dangle my legs off the lip. Of course, as disc golfers, we probably would dream all day about hucking a good one off the side but I understand that is frowned upon.

When we arrived at the North Rim of the canyon, there were ten travelers in the van, four were young teens. When the doors to the van opened, a cold rush of air entered and there was fog as far as the eye could see. The tour guide relayed back to us: "I don't know how good of a view we will get today, visibility is pretty low. Sorry about that. It's cold out there, better grab a jacket."

When I say cold, I mean we left Nevada where it was 104 degrees and here it was in the 30's, quite a drastic change. I grabbed my jacket and jumped out the door to hit the trail to the edge before anyone in the van could even find their hoodies, hats, or cameras. Two of the young people were on their phones and their parents told them to come out and join us, and much to my disbelief I heard them respond: "It's cold, and you can't see anything anyway!" The parents persevered and finally the kids reluctantly gave in.

On the edge of the canyon, the fog lifted and before my eyes was the third most beautiful thing I have ever seen. The first was my wife on our wedding day, the second was the birth of my son, and the third was this great wonder of the world massively stretched out before me. I sat on the edge of the canyon and nothing in the world seemed to matter. I forgot that I had a job, forgot that I had bills, forgot about all arguments I ever had with family or friends, and I certainly didn't feel the cold. All I felt was an immense state of gratitude for the immense beauty before me.

I heard the parents ask the kids what they thought. They still had their faces glued to their phones. "I think it's cold," one said. The other never responded because he couldn't hear them over his ear buds.

It sounds crazy, like this is an extreme example, but this is a metaphor for adults too. We miss so much beauty, so much of the moment, so much of this gift called life because we cannot tolerate a minutia of discomfort for relatively short periods of time.

This brings me to my conclusion. We have come to a point in our culture that we have become so used to the comfort of our homes, away from the elements, that anything outside of that zone seems unbearable. To put it simply, many people these days view any type of minor discomfort the same way they view pain. They will avoid anything that may seem remotely uncomfortable the same way they avoid personal injury to the extent that they would rather live in temperature controlled bubbles connected to a fake, pixelated, virtual reality and never open their eyes to see that this life is real and it is amazing! But here lies the secret: some of the best things you can experience in life happen outside of your comfort zone. They happen in the rain, in the snow, in the heat, in the fog, in the mud, in the dirt. We can always come back home, shower, dry off, and enjoy the safety and comfort of our homes, but what do we miss when we never venture out to hear the rain hitting the leaves or to make footprints in the snow?

Play disc golf while it's slightly raining? I'm there. The benefit just outweighs the excuse.

TAO TE "CHING!"
COMFORT AND PAIN

The absence of comfort
Is not the presence of pain

In the absence of comfort
We become absorbed in mindful presence

In the presence of comfort
We are conditioned to become ordinary

The habits of the ordinary
Do not lead to greatness

The habits of the ordinary
Lead straight to the grave

CHAPTER 11
TRICK YOURSELF INTO THROWING FARTHER

"To breakthrough your performance, you've got to breakthrough your psychology."

-Jensen Siaw

Of all the questions we have received over the last two
years at the *Zen Disc Golf Podcast*, nothing comes close
to the number of times we have been asked, "How can I
throw farther?" Of course, there have been many varia-
tions in the way this question has been asked, such as:

"What disc will fly the furthest?"
"How do I get my flick shot to go as far as
my backhand?"
"What grip method is best for power
shots?"

All of these questions ask the same thing: "How can I out-throw my buddy?"

In disc golf it is no mystery that being able to throw bombs straight down the fairway is not only one of the best ways to lower your score, but it also carries with it the feeling of absolute accomplishment. Watching your disc soar in the air farther than any of your competitors just plain feels good, and even more importantly, it can help set you up for a nice birdie putt.

This is the part where you may expect me to speak about the virtues of accuracy over power, because a tree or other obstacle doesn't really care how fast a disc is moving toward it – the harder it hits, the harder it falls. You might also expect me to speak about the virtues of developing a well-rounded game, to be more advantageous than spending most of your time trying to increase distance. Well, I have done that in other chapters and in the last book, so instead I am going to finally give a few tips that you might not hear very often on how to lengthen your drive and your accuracy.

These tips assume that your throwing technique is pretty much honed in, and that you are just trying to get that extra little bit of distance. You have been online watching YouTube clinics by pros (obviously this should be one of your first stops), and maybe even attended a drive clinic or two given locally by a bomb throwing pro. You have already asked your mentors for help and you might have even filmed your technique to make sure your X-step is on point, but you just can't breech your distance threshold.

After you have done all of this leg work and if you are still looking to throw just a little further, here is your tip: you may need to trick yourself into throwing that extra distance.

I play with a lot of new players, teaching them everything I know about this wonderful sport. About once a week I hit the course with a few new players, some playing for the first time, and we usually will play our course's short tee to short basket, as they begin learning the fundamentals. As some of the new players begin to pick up the game and begin developing a good throwing technique, they begin parring and birdieing more holes regularly. This is often when they ask me how to get that power drive, and my response is usually the same, *play the long tees.*

They look at me as if I have two heads. "I want to throw further to get closer to the basket, and you want me to move further away from the basket? That doesn't help me at all!" I tell them to just take my word for it. Over the next few rounds, we play the long tees and inevitably they land further from the basket than if we played the short tees and of course, their scores go up. Then I have them play the short tees again. It never fails, they begin parking their shots under baskets while adding 20 to 50ft to their drives!

Playing different courses, different tees, different baskets, etc. accomplishes multiple goals. It switches things up for you, breathing new life into your game. It forces you to step up your game to meet new challenges. It helps you to rid yourself of self-limiting beliefs such as, "On this hole I usually land my disc 20 foot from the basket, this sets me up for either a 20-foot putt or upshot." Then, because this is the limit you have in your mind - you achieve it. But, is it really an achievement?

Sometimes in life, we only set goals we believe are well within our reach and don't challenge ourselves to reach beyond them. The best way to get what we really want is to reach well beyond what we think is possible and head for the seemingly impossible. This way, even if we don't get 100% of what we want, we may get 90%, instead of settling for 70-80%.

One thing the fire academy taught me over a decade ago is that we all have more ability to push ourselves further than we ever initially think possible. *Thinking possible* is the key. Sometimes thinking isn't enough and we have to be forced to show ourselves what we are capable of. That may mean learning we can throw further by moving further away.

After a few rounds with my friends who are now throwing farther than me, they now want to play long tees to long baskets. Bunch of show offs.

TAO TE "CHING!"
POSSIBILITY

You can be more powerful
Than you think
But you are just as powerful
As you think

Step outside of yourself
See yourself not for who you are
But what you could be

If you believe something is impossible
You will prove it to yourself every time
If you believe something is possible
You will prove it to yourself every time

CHAPTER 12
A GAME OF RESPONSE,
NOT REACTION

"When you react, you are giving away your power. When
you respond, you are staying in control of yourself."

- Bob Proctor

The first thing most of us do when we step up onto a tee
pad is select our line of flight. We then choose a disc in
combination with a throw that should fly that line to get
us where we want to be in the fairway or the putting cir-
cle. This is where strategy in disc golf is so different than
regular golf (or ball golf). On non-par 3 holes in ball golf,
when you step up to a tee to make your initial shot you
will grab your main distance driving club of choice, usually a wood or driver that you are most comfortable with,
and your object is to smash your ball as far as you can
while keeping it on the fairway. In disc golf, the process

is a little different. Standing between us and our target are an array of obstacles such as trees, water, mandos, wind conditions, and other manmade objects. Shot selection off the tee becomes very important. This is not in any way to minimize ball golf, which has its own sets of obstacles, the thought process is just different. There is a little more strategy involved in shot shaping to get your disc where you need it to land, and even then you have to think ahead about your next shot as well.

So, when disc golfers step up to the tee box, especially on a new course, very often they are formulating a plan of attack on the hole. For newer players, this is a concept that might take a while to really sink in mentally, because it is easy to want to use the same strategy every time using a ball golf mentality. In other words, newer disc golfers see a hole in terms of feet or par and grab their biggest driver in attempt to power drive that disc as far as they can, hoping that the obstacles won't jump out and hit their disc. A seasoned player steps up on the tee with a different mentality. They see the obstacles as part of the game and use the tools, whether it is a throwing style or disc type, to "play the obstacles," holding also in their mind a plan for the next shot. With this line of thinking, distance becomes secondary to strategy. A flight line is chosen, a plan is made, and carefully the disc golfer throws the disc hoping that he has practiced enough that his throw is good and that his disc does what it has done for him so many other times.

The important point that I want to make is that choosing a line in disc golf and strategizing is responsive not reactionary. When I say this, I am defining the term 'reactionary' as a reflex to stimulus. Words that often accompany reaction are: backlash, backfire, compensation, counterbalance, kickback, and knee jerk. The word reaction has become attached to quickness, without thought, unconscious, and sometimes even forced by emotion.

Responsive, on the other hand, implies making conscious and deliberate choices. In this way, over time, when we arrive at the tee pad or at our disc after a second shot, the best way to view your shot is a response to your current situation, not a reaction. In order to lower your score, you must make conscious and deliberate shots and see strategy as a higher priority than mere distance. Throwing far can be important, and hopefully you learned some tricks to make that happen in the last chapter, but it takes a backseat to strategy. Once again, you can't out throw a poor decision.

We also see this in life. Ask yourself this question: Are you reacting life's circumstances or responding to them? Very often when we are faced with adversity or challenges in life our first line of defense is reactionary, without conscious reasoning or thought. This is a symptom of using our lower brains (also known as our limbic system) to encode and react to what is happening around us. It takes the brain much less energy to respond this way because it takes less thought. The limbic system will dump adrenaline into your blood stream, activating your fight or flight response. So, if someone throws a disc into your group but doesn't hit anyone and you become irate, running back to the tee box and cursing at them and telling them where they can shove their Aviar putters, is merely reacting to stimulus.

Responding involves using higher thinking and reasoning. Your limbic system may fire adrenaline but this is where you take that breath, or count to ten, and allow your neocortex (the reasoning and rationalizing part of your brain which separates humans from animals) to take over, and you might even come to the conclusion that maybe the next group couldn't even see your group on the thickly wooded course.

The key here is, before you react to anything in life or on the course, take a breath, allow your neocortex to go to work and respond to each new situation instead of once again, lobbing shot after shot merely reacting to your situation. It may only take that one breath to allow that higher processing and thinking take over to help you strategize, think outside of the box, and make better decisions. Find your line, choose your tool, take a deep breath, and just throw!

TAO TE "CHING!"
RESPONDING NOT REACTING

Respond
Don't react
With reaction
We lose control
With response
We gain control

With control
We stand above the masses
Lost and out of control

The obstacle
Is a step toward greatness
Not a wall of failure

You must see the gap and not just the trees

CHAPTER 13

A BASKET IS A GOAL,
A TEE IS THE FIRST STEP

"What you get by achieving your goals is not as important as what you become by achieving your goals."

- Henry David Thoreau

A tee pad is usually a concrete or rubber rectangle that only instructs us in one way: "Stand here for your first throw." Usually, the first thing we do on the tee pad is to look for the disc catcher to guide us in which direction to throw our disc. Without having a visual on the catcher or the ability to read proper signage, theoretically we could throw our disc in any direction we choose, but we don't. Because, we always take that first step in visualizing that basket.

Sometimes we can do this from the tee pad and sometimes we have to take a short walk down the fairway until we can develop a plan of action on the hole. We do this at least 18 times a round and overtime we may play hundreds and sometimes thousands of holes a year. But how often do we visualize and develop a plan of attack on our goals in life?

This idea jumped out at me this past week, sort of like a tree on one of the holes on my local course does in front of one of my fairway drivers. I may have noticed this before, but this time I really spent some time and meditated on the idea. There is often a gap between simply having a brief sense of something and paying attention it. That gap is called mindfulness.

You see, on the course, a basket represents a goal. And a tee pad represents where you are standing *right now*. The disc you choose, the grip you use, the type of throw you make are all for the most part being planned on that tee pad. In mere seconds, you have visualized a goal, taken your first step to reach that goal, and made a plan to get there. This is one of the many ways disc golf is just like life.

We set our sights on goals and move toward them hole after hole, and round after round, but do we do this at home or at work? How often do we step onto the tee pad of life and huck ourselves any direction we feel like, not paying any attention to want we want out of life, simply because it feels good to pick an open line (often the easiest line) and just throw?

Many times in life, we end up throwing in the opposite direction of our basket or goal, simply because we have no defined purpose, we are just throwing. Sounds ridiculous doesn't it? The basket is your purpose, without the basket you are just throwing. Likewise, what you want from life are your goals, but you must identify what you want, and develop a plan to get there, otherwise you are costing your life extra strokes.

A wise man once stated "If you fail to plan, then you plan to fail." This quote has been attributed to many famous thinkers over the years from Benjamin Franklin to Winston Churchill. What that means is that MANY great men through the ages have known a simple truth: To win at life you need to set a goal, have a plan, and take steps to achieve it. It is so basic, but it is the essence behind 98.999% of all successes in history. Okay, so I made that statistic up, but it would be impossible to refute, so I'm going to leave it in the book. The bottom line is this: most great things don't just happen, they are made to happen.

The basis of micro-economics is the assumption that people have unlimited wants. Very often, we all have great ideas how we can achieve these wants, but as soon as we have that great idea, our brain (and sometimes our peers) seems to want to tell us all the reasons we can't have it instead of help us outline a plan to get it. "It's too hard." "I don't have the time." "I don't have the knowledge or experience." "I don't want to make a sacrifice."

All these are lies we tell ourselves which hold us back in life. When you define what you want in life, you also need to ignore the voice in your head that tells you every reason why you can't be great. This little monster that lives in your head thrives on his ability to con you out of being amazing in order to keep you on the couch, guzzling gallons of ice cream and watching reruns of the Golden Girls, because it's simply easier than proving the little demon wrong.

Nothing is too hard to achieve, some things just take more time and persistence. It is true that if you are 4'10" tall, you cannot think yourself into being as tall as Shaquille O'neal, and slam dunking a basketball, but positive thinking has never hurt a single soul's drive to achieve. Negative thinking, on the other hand, eliminates the drive of millions of people to achieve daily.

Oh, and about not having enough time to reach for what you want: If you are alive all you have is time. Time is life. You just need to budget it like you would (or should) budget your bank account. Every person on this earth is given the gift of 1,440 minutes a day, 365 days a year. At the completion of this book, I would have spent approximately 100 hours, over a two year period, equaling approximately 0.006% of my life over two years. That equates to about 8.6 minutes a day, and people constantly ask me: "How on Earth did you find time to write a book?" Facebook steals about 50 minutes a day from most Americans according to a recent poll. If that doesn't sound like a big number, using the figures above, I could have possibly written almost 6 books per year, within the time someone else hits "like" on a new cat meme or share's another article about how sugar is bad for you. We get it, thumbs down sugar. I'm on a tangent.

By budgeting time, I wrote this book and because I was able to do this, I make part of my living off of what I love, disc golf. You can do the same thing. Budget your time, set a goal, and take action to get better at disc golf, write that novel you have always wanted to write, learn a new language, or a speed metal solo on the banjo. You cannot make time, but you can waste it.

TAO TE "CHING!"
GOALS

A goal is worthless
Without a plan.

Many people have goals
Very few have plans.

CHAPTER 14
AGGRESSIVE VS FINESSE PLAY

"Make haste slowly."

- Benjamin Franklin

There is no doubt about it, as we have already previously mentioned, all disc golfers want more distance on their drives. That's part of the quest for higher speed distance drivers, more glide, and techniques that allow us to whip a disc like Simon Lizzote, effortlessly putting our favorite drivers out there, 300 to 400 feet or even farther. But let's be really honest here- not every hole allows for that type of power and the most experienced player will tell you that if you have a tight gap between obstacles that you need to thread; power, speed, and aggression are not necessarily your best friends. On tight shots, finesse is a better ally.

The word 'finesse' has French origins and is derived

from the word 'fine,' when you are describing something pure and delicate. Webster's Dictionary defines finesse as follows:

> FINESE: Skill and cleverness that is shown in the way someone deals with a situation or problem.

To put it another way, finesse means evaluating a situation for what it is, and instead of using the same tools (discs) or tricks (types of throws) that you might normally use, you use the *correct* tools or tricks for the job. In order to evaluate the situation, you must be immersed in it and be able to visualize all possible tools, tricks, and outcomes (shots).

Think about it as if you are some type of disc golf Terminator and have a cyborg-like lens in front of your vision, constantly drawing geometrical shapes and lines and coming up with figures overtop of your view of the shot. It runs through a sequence of possibilities carefully but quickly, and assists you in finding the best shot you could possibly take. In order for the system to work though, it has to overlay your current shot and not the last one or the next one. To evaluate your current situation you need to be absorbed in it. This is called meditative focus. Breaking that down:

Meditation is absorption in the now.
Focus is meditation in action.

Having a sense of meditative focus allows you to step out of the box and make game based decisions rather than ego based decisions.

By game based decisions, I mean what action or shot will work best right now and improve your overall score. By ego based decisions, I mean what shot merely makes you feel or look better than someone else. In this way you are playing the course, not your competition. In essence, sometimes that means throwing a putter off the tee, taking a stroke, and setting yourself up for a distance shot which you are more comfortable with throwing. Sometimes it means playing par golf instead of always going for the birdie. Sometimes it means not putting 100% of your power on a faster disc, or maybe "discing" down altogether. That's what it means to make game based over ego based decisions.

Finesse is to game based decisions, what aggression is to ego based decisions. Therefore, disc golf is inherently more a game of finesse than a game of aggression. That is not to say that aggression cannot be harnessed when that is the right move to play, but it is less likely that this technique will work. Watch pro disc golfers on the tee. They make whipping a driver 500 ft look effortless, almost as if they are playing in slow motion on the tee. This is because they have learned that technique over power is the key to throwing these wonderful round pieces of plastic.

This is just like life. Every obstacle, conflict, wall we find ourselves up against is not always a prescription for us to handle with aggression. Newton's 3rd law of motion is not only true in physics but also in human interaction:

> For every action, there is an equal and
> opposite reaction.

This means that any energy you put into this world is returned to you equally and in the opposite direction. Most often, when we find ourselves in conflict, the answer is not to respond aggressively but to respond intelligently, with finesse. Responding aggressively only makes the opposition dig in their heels and fight back tooth and nail. This is why Socrates believed the Socratic method was the best way to have an effective debate with others. He would not argue at all. He would merely ask his opponent questions until they found the errors in their own logic.

There is an old analogy in Taoist philosophy which states that when you reach a rockslide in the middle of the road that makes travel impossible for you to cross or go around, you should become like water finding all of cracks to get to the other side rather than expelling all your energy pushing, pulling, or punching (ouch!) the rockslide aggressively. To be like water means to go with the flow and finding the cracks is using that flow to find the weakness of an obstacle.

On the disc golf course this is using meditative focus to make game based decisions instead of ego based decisions. In life it is the same, finding the delicate flow that gets you to the other side.

TAO TE "CHING!"
THE RIGHT TOOLS

The right tool
The right method
The right outcome

The wrong tool
The wrong method
The wrong outcome

Never assemble
Fine porcelain
With a hammer

CHAPTER 15
HOW TO GROW THE SPORT

"The future depends on what you do today."

- Ghandi

In this chapter, I would like to talk to you about how we are going to grow this great sport of disc golf, but first I want to talk to you about something I call "investments in the spirit." I introduced this term in my last book and I identified this concept as any activity you do that only requires small amounts of time or resources which you give to others and that eventually come back to you with a much higher return than the effort you initially gave.

I want you to picture yourself as a vessel that holds all the good things you want out of life. This vessel grows as you receive more and more of the good stuff. I am talking about love, affection, friendship, wisdom, fun, but also success and money. There is room for all of this good stuff in your vessel. That is, until it gets full.

Now what I want you to understand about this vessel is that it can always grow to allow for more of the good stuff. There really is no limit to how much it can grow, but at a certain point of filling this vessel, its growth begins to stagnate. It begins to slow down and stops letting more good stuff in.

The good news is there is a secret to get you through that stagnation so your vessel can continue to grow to get more of what you want out of life. This secret may sound a little counterintuitive but hear me out:

You have to let some of that good stuff out!

That's right, you have got to make a little space in that vessel to let the universe know that you are ready to be refilled again and to grow some more. You have got to give away some of that good stuff and have faith that it not only will be returned, but it will be returned with more abundance.

So, if you want more love, you're going to have to be more loving. If you want more affection you're going to have to be more affectionate. If you want more friends, you will need to be a better friend to the ones you already have. If you want more wisdom, you're gonna have to teach others. If you want more success you're going to have to help other people find their success. And if you want more money (which all of us really do), you're going to have to let some money go (to the cause of your choice) with unrelenting faith that it is going to come back to you.

It is no secret that over the past two years, I have been in the position to give a lot of things away through social media and the podcast. I am often asked how I can afford to give so many things away. The answer is simple: for everything I give away, I get back at least tenfold from you guys and girls, my listeners, readers, and followers. Therefore, my small investments reap much higher rewards than their initial dollar values.

But let me explain this to you: Your return on investment is not going to come immediately. Sometimes it takes time. Sometimes we have been *taking* for so long that we have to let a lot out of our vessels before we can start *receiving* again. But when you start getting it back, it will be no mystery as to why it has come back into your life.

This law of giving, (and it is a law) works every time, but unfortunately, as we get so wrapped up in our own lives, it becomes very easy to get into the habit of taking more than we give.

As our vessel becomes full, it won't allow any more good

stuff to get in. In fact, with a lack of gratitude and appreciation for what we already have, the vessel begins to shrink and actually pushes some good stuff out and we become self-destructive. We spend more than we make, we go into debt, taking more than we give. We eat more calories than we burn, we get fat, taking more than we give. We expect more out of others, without giving them more of ourselves. We cause our own suffering, taking more than we give.

Now don't misunderstand me. You don't need to empty your vessel in order to get more out of life. In other words, you don't have to donate all of your money or all of your time to expect better results out of life. It actually takes very little to get the process going and it is not all about money as I mentioned above.

As a matter of fact, the easiest way for you to give is to use the talents that you already have to make the world a better place.

There is an old Zen proverb that tells of a student going to his master and asking him, "How can we bring about world peace?" Unexpectedly, the Zen master simply says, "Sweep the floor." You see, it is not always the big things we do that make huge differences. The little things that we do every day help make our lives better and other people's lives better as well. That then multiplies and makes the world a better place.

So how does this relate to growing the sport of disc golf? We often talk about "growing the sport" and the reason we want to do this is because disc golf gives so much to us. It is fun, peaceful, meditative, and we enjoy the competition. And often it is not necessary to invest much money to play. It gives us so much and yet expects so little.

If you truly want to grow the sport of disc golf, you are going to have to plant some seeds that will grow disc golf. When we talk about planting seeds, we aren't just talking about money. You can just as easily grow the sport using any talent that you already have:

- Donate your time to other people, teaching them how to play.
- If you're talented at working with children, develop a program to get children involved in disc golf.
- Sacrifice some of your game time to collect trash on the course.
- If you're a writer: start a blog or write a book! Even if you don't have any web development skills, help by contributing your articles to blogs already in existence.
- If you are good at landscaping, volunteer to assist with course maintenance.

- If you are good at organizing, organize a league or team for your college, school, job, or organize a club for your locality.
- If you are good at photography, show the world the beauty that you see on the disc golf course. (don't forget to post to Twitter and Instagram with the tag #zendiscgolf)

Your options are limitless. We all have talents that, if used with the right amount of focus, will not only grow the sport but will make the world a better place.

TAO TE "CHING!"
RIGHT ACTION

Talents are gifts
Cultivated to convert

Passion to occupation
Time to money
Learning to wisdom
Seeds to trees
Existence to living
Recreation to athleticism
A game to a sport

Use your talents to
Spread this game

And…

Just
Keep
Throwing.

CHAPTER 16
A ZEN CONVERSATION

A written conversation between
Tim Steward and Patrick McCormick
January 2015

Tim: Patrick, I can't tell you how much I dig *Zen & the Art of Disc Golf.* It must be really cool to have a book out with your name on it. Especially one that is getting as much traction in the community as this one is. As a wannabe writer myself, I can kind of relate to what an undertaking it must have been.

Patrick: Thanks Tim. It is really cool. And to be quite honest, I had no idea that the whole thing would take off like it has. I am insanely grateful for the success that is happening, but what makes it even better is that a positive message is spreading and people are eating it up and that means even more to me than any kind of personal success. Money comes and goes, but ideas endure. I have so many books that have impacted me over the years and that still impact my daily thinking. To think that maybe my book is impacting even one person's daily thoughts positively is incredible to me.

Tim: I agree. I can't seem to read enough and I always scratch my head a little when people tell me they don't read. I always think that it's because their only exposure to reading stemmed from bad teachers forcing books on them that didn't interest them. It's crazy how many people got soured on reading that way. I've always got a little internal mission to get people to read more by exposing them to the right books. For me, I have a list of books that I recommend all the time. *Striking Thoughts* by Bruce Lee, *The War of Art* by Steven Pressfield, and *On the Shortness of Life* by Seneca are all personal favorites. I'm also a huge fiction fan. Neil Gaiman, William Gibson, and Tim Powers are my top three.

I noticed that you have a pretty solid bibliography in the back of your book. If you were to select 2 to 3 of those as must reads for your audience, which would they be? What book do you suggest to people who say, "I don't read"?

Patrick: I guess "must reads" would depend on what you are searching for. *Be Here Now* by Ram Dass is a visual masterpiece and gives an overview of many different spiritual concepts and ideas. *Embraced by the Light* by Betty J. Eadie is a book about one woman's very vivid near death experience that I believe is an absolutely beautiful account of what we should be doing here on Earth, as well as many things we shouldn't be. For those who say they "don't read," it's all about finding something that interests you. I think we have all looked something up on Wikipedia and that led to clicking link after link. The brain is naturally a sponge. People who don't read just haven't found something that interests them enough to get them started.

Tim: One of the things that always strikes me as ironic is that most of the things that grow our sport don't involve actually playing our sport. I know for me, I give up a lot of playing time to write this blog, keep up the Instagram and Twitter feeds, and do other disc golf related projects.

It's so hard to have the self discipline, especially on a really nice day, to not spend my whole day playing when I know I have writing to do. What was your motivation to stay disciplined in the process? How did you have the self control and drive to give up a thing you clearly love so much to write this book?

Patrick: To tell you the truth this book took so long because I would go through periods of really focused writing, then life would happen, and it would be set aside for a while. Then all of a sudden I would hit the course and the have some small revelation and would often either take a quick note or drop everything I was doing to leave the course and write about it. I believe the secret to productivity is routine. I was far more productive when I kept a disciplined routine.

I have always been a project oriented person. I love the feeling of completing something that I can be proud of. It's sort of a high that I chase. I hate having unfinished things out there. Sometimes I involve other people, and promise completion to ensure that I actually will complete something. In this case social networking was my go to. As I continued to promote an unfinished book, adding more and more people to Instagram and Facebook, I felt like I was promising more people a product. Even though those people had no idea, I continued the project because I felt like I owed them something. I also thanked many of those people in the back of my book.

Tim: Ah the power of a routine! I'm actually going to be writing a blog post about that sometime soon. In addition to just finding time, having a routine, and just plain sacrifice, I'm guessing a component of that question is how did you find your "Why?" Without a strong *why*, none of that can be very effective. How can our fellow disc golfer find their "*why*" for the things they want to do in their lives? I think that applies not only to writing books and playing disc golf, but across most of people's goals and aspirations.

Patrick: As human beings, we are always looking for "why." For me it was the idea that maybe something I had to say could improve other people's lives. Why keep something like that a secret? So I guess you could say instead of asking why I asked "Why not?" In the end, people read it or they don't. They get it or they don't. But even if it only impacts a single person, then why not do my part and give it a shot.

In my book, I talk about leaving everything better than you found it. It is a principle I try to live by and knowing than I cannot live forever, the only thing I can leave leave behind is a legacy. Why not try to make it great?

Tim: That's really cool that you put it that way. I know a lot of super successful people that I read about say they start with the legacy in mind and that shapes their day to day decisions. What is that old saying? Something like "A person is not truly dead until their name crosses the lips of a living person for the last time?" I guess we all have such a limited amount of time on this Earth that it is pretty important to do something meaningful with it.

Patrick: That's a great way to put it.

Tim: With your career choice and the things you have said so far, it seems like you have a sincere desire to really help as many other people as you can. One of my favorite people, Zig Ziglar, is most well known for saying, "You can have anything in life you want if you just help enough other people get what they want."

Patrick: The most important part of that is understanding it is not a tit for tat. The universe doesn't OWE you anything.

Tim: You are so right about that! You do for others merely for the sake of doing for others. Then and only then does the universe return the favor. It wasn't until I got older that I really started to grasp how true that was. It's a really rare and admirable quality and I'm always curious how people get it. So many people never do and they go through life totally self centered. You see that on the disc golf course all the time. Some people really root for everyone they are playing with and others wish for you to hit a tree. I think that the attitude on the course is such a good indicator of how they treat everyone in their life. Was an attitude of service to others instilled in you by your parents, have you always had it or did you get it another way?

Patrick: An attitude of service was instilled in me very slowly. It wasn't one thing or one person. It was just the realization that "As you give, you shall be given to." You just sort of start seeing it happen in your life and in people's lives around you. Watch how people live. See if the things they are doing are making them happy or miserable. You can always trace it to their daily attitudes.

Tim: So I think all of this leads to one of my favorite hot button topics. Taking care of our courses. I was absolutely thrilled to see you devote some time in your book to this. This is one of my soap box topics and I'm super passionate about it. Not just in the basic stuff like picking up after yourself, hitting the garbage can, picking up garbage you see left around, and not breaking stuff. But also in club work days.

Patrick: Taking care of our courses is on the top of the list of things that are going to grow this sport. We must show people the beauty this game has to offer in order for them to see it is not all about lobbing "frisbees" in the woods. This is one of the reasons why I try to share a beautiful disc golf image every day on my Instagram and Facebook, hoping people share with others and show them the beauty that a disc golf course has to offer. Taking care of the course begins with the people playing the course. Clubs do great jobs of assisting and maintaining, but even one day a week of maintenance can't keep up with six days of destruction.

Tim: I, unfortunately, end up working during most of our club work days, but I know we have a semi-hard time getting any good number of people to show up for them. I also know our club is not alone in that regard. But even outside of formally organized work days, there are other things people can do. I know I'll grab a garbage bag or two once a week and just pick up as much trash as I can find in a round.

Patrick: Taking pride and ownership. That is number one. Treat the course as if it is your home. I would hope you just don't throw trash in your yard, or destroy lawn furniture you paid for. Take some responsibility for your course. You may not have trashed it, but if you can fix it, do it!

Tim: Why do you think it's so difficult to get the bulk of the disc golfers out there to embrace this concept? Is it a large global problem, or is it just a handful of inconsiderate people who make the rest of us look bad? What do you think are some possible solutions to this?

Patrick: When people do not have "skin in the game" it is easier for them to destroy. This is just going to be the nature of a low cost to enter sport. I'm not advocating that it shouldn't be, but it is a fact – people who don't have skin in the game or do not take pride and ownership in something also do not respect it. You and I, we respect disc golf. It's hard for us to imagine trashing a course. Sometimes the course is trashed by non-disc golfers and sometimes it is merely something to do while you enjoy other not-so-legal activities. Either way it's difficult to say what the answer is. But the development of pride and ownership in general is the key.

A SHOWING OF GRATITUDE

Thank you.

This is crazy. That is the only way I can describe the feeling of completing a second book detailing disc golf as a metaphor for living well. With this book, I am standing on the tee pad visualizing chains. The first book was a blind ace. This one, I obviously hope will be the same.

I would not be standing here, this time, if I was standing alone. Their are many people who deserve a 10 ton bag of credit for this book. Keep reading, you may recognize many of these names:

Chris, my lovely wife. She has stood with me and held me up for almost six years now. She is the unsung hero in the Zen Disc Golf movement. Though she does not play, she deserves a massive amount of credit for being the biggest cheerleader for my writing, podcasting, and disc golf in general. She even let me move our family to the middle of nowhere, so that I could live out my dream - living on my own course. I love you. I could not have done this without you.

Zach Engelhart, Tim Steward, and Chris Bawden. The 3 co-hosts of the Zen Disc Golf Podcast - The three of you all entered my life through disc golf and gave up massive amounts of time and energy to see this thing grow. I cherish your friendships more than you could know.

All of the guests of the Zen Disc Golf Podcast: Alan Barker (Infinite Discs), Jeremy Zaborowsky (Chain Cutters Union), Jason Mason and Chris Kelley (Good Up Disc Golf), Alan Hargreaves, Matt Krueger (uDisc App), Joshua Keith (Therapy Disc Golf), Alan Musselman (Tribaloid), John Heaton (St. Jude Invitational Director), David Mawr, Megan Nance (Yoga for Disc Golf), Garin Wootton (Black Zombie Disc Golf), David Tucker (Big Daddy Disc Golf), Steve Dodge (Vibram Disc Golf), Ryan "Slim" Pickens and Justin Menickelli (*The Definitive Guide to Disc Golf* book)

Corporate sponsors of the Zen Disc Golf Podcast: Infinite Discs, Appalachian Disc Golf, Audible, and Discmania.

Individual sponsors of the Zen Disc Golf Podcast: Joel Voss, Kenneth Rogers, Ryan Boyd, Adam Gowland, Calvin Negrete, 307 Disc Golf, Kevin Kugler, SMD, Joel Bautista, Seth Jensen, Benjamin Wonders, Roger Crain, Timmy Andersson, Jared Wiglusz, Todd Sisco, Royal Daniel, Alan Kendrick, Melissa Martin, Scott Comeaux, Jeremy Ziakas, Ryan Lewis, Christopher Moen Pettersen, Lynn Henriksen, Christopher Strum, Jorn Idar Kvig, and Scott Seagle.

Zen Disc Golf Team Box backers: Matt Fluture, Steven Hadley, Ian Jarvis, Kasey Joe, Chris Wallen, Jeff Glynn, Randy, Alan Hargreaves, Daryl Stonemason, Tim, Jeremy Zaborowski, Jamie, Micha Rollnik, Ola Hagbohm, Kevin Kugler, Jeremy Ziakis, Kasey Wolf, Richard Clark, Talyn Christopher Strum, Donald Ferris, Lynn Henriksen, Doug Langford, Rodney Lane, Travis, Dane, Rob Hosely, Jon Gensel, Jeremy Leadbetter, Kyle Eno, Josh Williams, Michael Barnes & Noble, Jack McGuigan, Matt Marvaldi, Roger Crain, April Bishop Burkhart, Kelby Bales, Seth Jensen, Sue Graham, Timm Desouza, Eric Hermann, Ron McIlroy, Sam I., Andrew Denman, Jennifer Regan, Nathan Meece, Douglas Baker, Jeremiah Rau, Alan, Lee Gregory, Jon-Paul Lussier Jr., Maxwell Perna, Caitlin Cobb, Jim Quinn, Dakota Johnston, Brandon Tougaw, Nicholas Bordwell, Alex T. Sperley, Greg De La Rosa III, John J Tucker, Andrew Hincks,

Will Hancock, Shadrach Nutting, Curtis, Benjamin C. Wonders, Peter Epperson, Kevin Johnson, Kyle Van Houtte, Rob, Chris Siepert, Joe Martin, Andrew Aleshire, William Paschal, Tyler McBrian, Elliot Story, Troy LaMont, Terrass Misher, Susan Lamon Wallen, Joshua Phillips, Aaron, Chuck, Anthony Galvan, Scott McHale, Ed Lee Grimm, Joe Ellison, Michael Brundis, Ray Saltrelli, Jane Snyder, Steve W., Jared Wiglusz, Blair Van Velse, Chris Mahaffey, Drew Frost, Jeffrey Allen, Chris Bawden, Marc Lyspen, Mark Heydt, Jason Mather, Paul McMican, Mark Pruett, Jeremy Sneeden, Greg Schneider Jr., Jacob Warren, John Kenny, Diane Berkovatz, and Jason Narf Hibben

Last but not least I'd like to thank **my regular DG crew**. The source of so much fun and inspiration - John Berry, Brandon Guethe, Tommy and Carmen Brosam, Jasper Guitierez, Herman Kappes, Greg Deiterich, Derek Gundersen, Matt Payne, Ryan Norman, Jeff Berry, and Bryce Atlas McCormick

Thank YOU for reading!

TAO TE "CHING" INDEX